Illustrated Living History Series

HOME BUILDING AND WOODWORKING

IN COLONIAL AMERICA

C. Keith Wilbur

Chelsea House Publishers

Philadelphia

First published in hardback edition in 1997 by Chelsea House Publishers.

1 3 5 7 9 8 6 4 2

Library of Congress Cataloging-in-Publication Data

Wilbur, C. Keith, 1923-
Homebuilding and woodworking in colonial America / C. Keith Wilbur.
p.   cm.-- (Illustrated living history)
Includes bibliographical references and index.
ISBN 0-7910-4529-3
1. House construction--United States--History--16th century.
2. Building, Wooden--United States--History--16th century.
3. Carpentry--United States--History--16th century. I. Title.
II.Series.
TH4809.U6W55 1996
690'.837'097409033--dc20
                                            96-42336
                                              CIP

Contents

PREFACE

The 1750 Cape had known happier days. In the cold November light, it was clear that the back ell and much of the rear roof had been burned beyond repair. Our son Bruce had bought the house at a fire-sale price from the discouraged owner. Looking beyond the charred hewn boards, it had that time-aged friendliness of colonial architecture. Incidentally, one of the finest trout streams in Connecticut flowed through the property. On Thanksgiving day, the family gathered to protect the remains of the house from the coming winter snows. Our traditional turkey dinner lost out to a pot of home-brewed stew, cooked in a fireplace that had served other New Englanders for over three centuries.

As we sat around the table— actually a door propped up on boxes— we couldn't help but admire the smoke-darkened wall panels, the graceful moldings, and the hand-wrought hardware. These memorials to the skills of some unsung colonial house-wright were entitled to a proper restoration.

In the months that followed, all who lent a hand became familiar with the handtools of an earlier America. All but lost in the pages of history, such practical knowhow deserves a retelling. And so I'd like to share with you my admiration for those pre-Revolutionary builders who could transform a stand of trees into a handsome homestead. I'd also like to think that they would give the newly restored Cape a nod of approval.

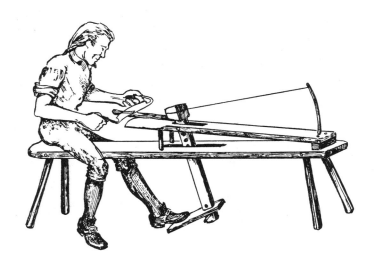

A WEALTH OF WOOD

Newcomers to America must have been astounded by the magnificent forests that crowded the settlements. Back in overpopulated, land-stripped Europe, the countryside had long since contributed the last of her virgin trees. In some countries, it was a hanging offense to level any remaining tree without permission. But in the colonies, virgin timber grew in quantity. These giants reached such heights that the lower branches received little of the light that filtered down from the canopy of leaves. Losing out, they fell off the trunk before fully developing. The result was a tall, straight, limb-free (and therefore knot-free) trunk that reached for the sun.

The most spectacular tree was the white pine. The timber soared to 150 feet and on up to 200 feet. Although a softer wood, the heartwood of these ancient pines was far more hard and dense than their smaller relatives of today. The English Navy claimed any white pine 2 feet or more in diameter for mast trees and had the trunk blazed with the King's broad arrow. The colonists, well on the way to becoming independent spirits in the new land, were not particularly troubled about using some of the huge timber for their own purposes. At any rate, wood in such plenty was the favorite building material in America.

THE KING'S
BROAD ARROW

There were other alternatives, for this new land was also rich with stone and clay for bricks. In all the colonies, such masonry made strong, durable foundations and chimneys. While wooden-framed houses continued to be the over-whelming choice in New England, the two more southerly colonies found brick homes much to their liking. The more elegant the structure, the more probable that it would be of brick. In Pennsylvania and the Hudson River Valley, stonework became more and more common. But the very workable and versatile woods had an appeal (which continues today) that was not to be denied.

THE VIRGIN
WHITE (OR PUMPKIN)
PINE TREE

1

A CHOICE OF DESIGNS

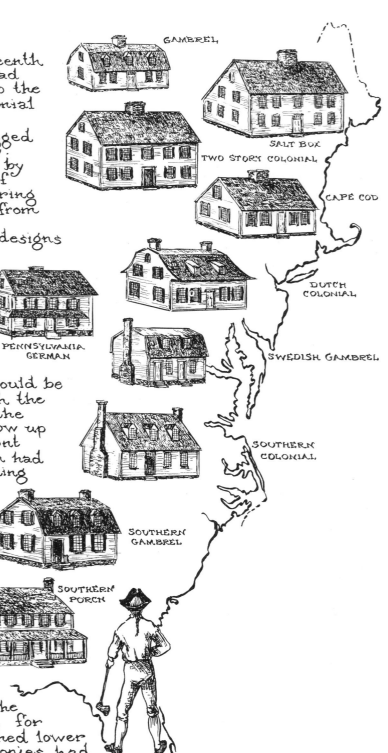

By the middle of the eighteenth century, American architecture had come into its own. By adapting to the conditions at hand, the early colonial homestead had developed its own personality ~ a happy blend of rugged construction and graceful simplicity. Regional designs were influenced by climate, preference, availability of building materials, and a smattering of traditional designs imported from the mother country.

In New England, original designs included the Cape Cod, a compact dwelling under a rather high-pitched roof that could meet the offshore storms on their own terms. By adding a second floor, the Two Story Colonial gave added room and flow of warmth from the downstairs fireplaces. As the family continued to grow, a back shed could be added to make the Salt Box. With the long, slanted roof facing north, the blustery winds of winter would blow up and over, while the two~story front collected whatever warmth the sun had to offer. Although the space~creating Gambrel roof was European, the settlers adapted its double slope to cap many Cape Cods and two~story colonials.

The middle colonials had their own version of the gambrel roof. The distinctive Dutch Colonial (actually of Flemish origin) carried the sweeping eaves well beyond the front and rear walls and dotted the Hudson River Valley on down into northern New Jersey. Beyond, along the Delaware watershed, the Swedish newcomers were known for their flat upper and steeply pitched lower gambrel roofs. The southern colonies had gambrels similar to those in New England, built in the traditions of their English ancestors.

GAMBREL

SALT BOX

TWO STORY COLONIAL

CAPE COD

PENNSYLVANIA GERMAN

DUTCH COLONIAL

SWEDISH GAMBREL

SOUTHERN COLONIAL

SOUTHERN GAMBREL

SOUTHERN PORCH

WOODS FOR POST-AND-BEAM FRAMING

Beneath the clapboard and shingle skin of every wooden homestead was a rugged skeleton. Great squared timbers made up the perpendicular posts and horizontal beams. They were forever joined by wooden tree nails ("trunnels"). Some of these framing members ran as large as 10 inches by 10 inches on cross-section—something of an over-kill for a house. To keep the posts square with the beams, braces were locked aslant between them. No doubt about it—the colonial homestead was built for the ages.

The builder's choice of timber for framing was certainly white oak. The majority of the early American colonists were English and they were well acquainted with its badly depleted relative, the English or Norman oak. They found the native oak all that they could wish, for it was very workable, strong, hard, and heavy, and held enough tannic acid in its fibers to discourage a number of fungi and insects. The tree was found in plenty throughout the eastern part of the country.

THIS WHITE OAK IN NEW HOPE, PENNSYLVANIA, WAS A DECADE OLD WHEN COLUMBUS DISCOVERED THE CARIBBEAN ISLANDS.

Some of these eastern trees also found their way into the timber framing:

RED MAPLE
HARD, HEAVY, STRONG; HARD TO WORK, AND TWISTS ON DRYING

RED OAK
WORKS WELL, LIGHTER THAN WHITE OAK; HARD TO SEASON AND DOES NOT RESIST DECAY

CHESTNUT
WORKS NICELY, FAIRLY SOFT, LIGHT, STRAIGHT-GRAINED, RESISTS MOISTURE AND FINE FOR DAMP SPOTS SUCH AS SILLS; NOW LOST COMPLETELY TO THE ASIAN CHESTNUT BLIGHT

WHITE OAK
EASILY WORKED; HARD, STRONG, HEAVY, RESISTS DECAY

HEMLOCK
WORKS WELL; BRITTLE, SPLINTERY, KNOTTY

WHITE PINE
WORKS WELL, SEASONS NICELY; LIGHT, KNOTTY

3

TOOLS FOR FRAMING

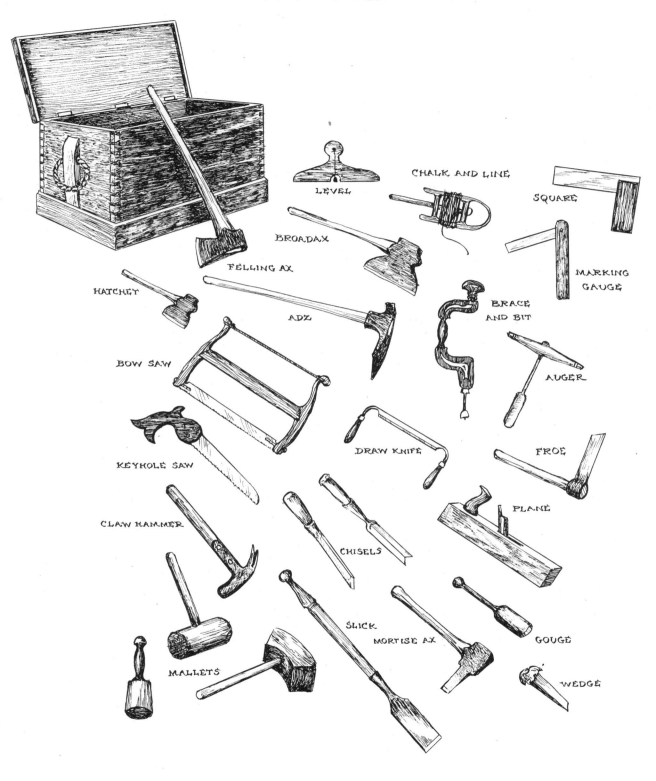

LEVEL

CHALK AND LINE

SQUARE

BROADAX

FELLING AX

MARKING GAUGE

HATCHET

ADZ

BRACE AND BIT

AUGER

BOW SAW

DRAW KNIFE

FROE

KEYHOLE SAW

CHISELS

PLANE

CLAW HAMMER

SLICK

GOUGE

MALLETS

MORTISE AX

WEDGE

4

THE FELLING AX

BUTT   HAFT OR HANDLE   POLL   BLADE   EYE   KNIFE EDGE

THE TRADE AX BEFORE 1740

No one tool could tame the American wilderness as did the felling ax. It cleared the forests to make way for the colonial homes and villages, then began the conversion of the felled trees into framing timber for the buildings. The Indian neighbors watched with amazement as those sharp-edged iron axes laid low the forest giants. Every right-thinking tribesman had to have just such a laborsaver for his own. Almost overnight, the trade ax brought the natives out of their Stone Age past and into the European advances of that day.

The formation of the trade ax was simplicity itself:

AN IRON STRAP WAS HEATED WHITE HOT ON THE FORGE.

THE ENDS WERE POUNDED INTO SHAPE.

THE FORGING OF THE EYE

A PIECE OF STEEL WAS WELDED INTO THE CUTTING EDGE. CLOSE INSPECTION CAN USUALLY DETECT THE WELD LINE RUNNING DOWN FROM THE EYE.

The colonial woodcutters had less enthusiasm for the trade ax than did the Indians. Perhaps it had served well enough in the depleted woodlands of Europe, but America's wealth of wood demanded a more efficient tool. The concentration of weight in the blade caused the axhead to wobble in the middle of a swing. Power and accuracy were lost. It was time to call up some Yankee ingenuity.

THE "AMERICAN" AX

There was a solution: Shift the weight, usually up to six pounds, to the center of the axhead. A chunk of iron was forged to the top of the trade ax eye. The process flattened the oval into a triangular eye. The blade was shortened to lessen the excessive heft. Extended ears gave added holding power to the handle and increased the weight to the middle. Only the handle remained the same — a sturdy straight rod of springy hickory.

Between 1725 and 1750, the new American pattern had become the favorite throughout the colonies. This ax proved so efficient that it remains essentially the same as that used today.

5

FROM TREE TO TIMBER

Like a giant supermarket for wood in the raw, the virgin American forests offered the best of timber for whatever the purpose. The trees grew straight and tall in their effort to reach the sun. Such intense competition to outreach their neighbors left the lower branches in deep shade. When still spindly, they would drop off to leave a clean trunk without troublesome knots.

CYLINDRICAL STEMS FROM A DENSE OVERSTORY

CONICAL STEMS GROWN IN THE OPEN

The woodsman shouldered his ax with the coming of the winter months when sap was no longer flowing. Old-timers hold that warm weather ferments a felled tree like apple juice mellowing into hard cider. The surplus of alcohol flowing in the sapwood circulation (or in humans for that matter) was followed by decay of the fibers. Not so with the pines, however, for the pitchy sap prevented the fermentation process. After felling, it was worth drying the log for a few days to avoid gumming up the hewing ax.

The first swing of the ax began the business of building the post-and-beam framework. But before that could happen, the practiced eye of the woodsman had to make several judgments.

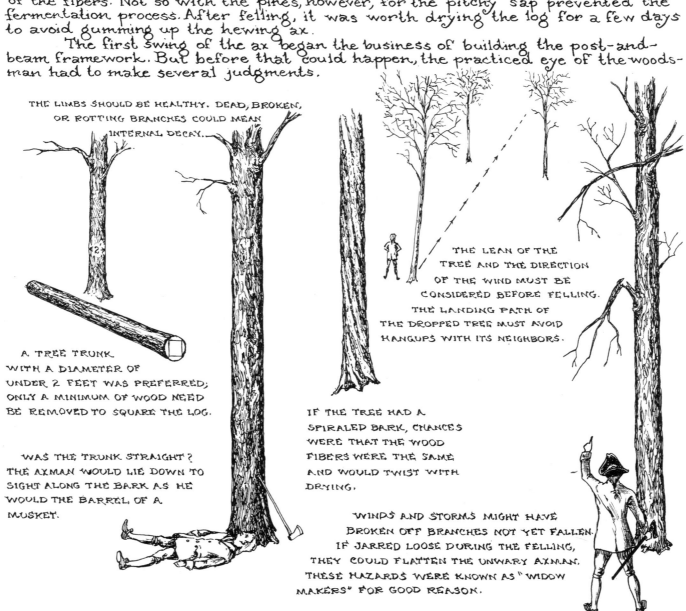

THE LIMBS SHOULD BE HEALTHY. DEAD, BROKEN, OR ROTTING BRANCHES COULD MEAN INTERNAL DECAY.

A TREE TRUNK WITH A DIAMETER OF UNDER 2 FEET WAS PREFERRED; ONLY A MINIMUM OF WOOD NEED BE REMOVED TO SQUARE THE LOG.

WAS THE TRUNK STRAIGHT? THE AXMAN WOULD LIE DOWN TO SIGHT ALONG THE BARK AS HE WOULD THE BARREL OF A MUSKET.

THE LEAN OF THE TREE AND THE DIRECTION OF THE WIND MUST BE CONSIDERED BEFORE FELLING. THE LANDING PATH OF THE DROPPED TREE MUST AVOID HANGUPS WITH ITS NEIGHBORS.

IF THE TREE HAD A SPIRALED BARK, CHANCES WERE THAT THE WOOD FIBERS WERE THE SAME AND WOULD TWIST WITH DRYING.

WINDS AND STORMS MIGHT HAVE BROKEN OFF BRANCHES NOT YET FALLEN. IF JARRED LOOSE DURING THE FELLING, THEY COULD FLATTEN THE UNWARY AXMAN. THESE HAZARDS WERE KNOWN AS "WIDOW MAKERS" FOR GOOD REASON.

FELLING ~ TIME TO SWING INTO ACTION

THE ORDER OF CUTS

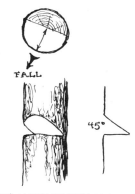

FALL

45°

LEFT HANDERS, OF COURSE, REVERSED THIS POSITION.

THE OBJECT WAS TO MAKE A DEEP HINGE ON THE SIDE WHERE THE TREE WAS TO FALL. THE FIRST THREE BLOWS CUT ON THE HORIZONTAL. THE RIGHT HAND, ARM COCKED BACK, HELD THE AX JUST BELOW THE HEAD. THE LEFT HAND, WITH ARM STRAIGHT ACROSS THE CHEST, GRASPED THE END OF THE HANDLE. THE SWING BROUGHT THE RIGHT HAND EVEN TO MEET THE LEFT.

WITH THE FIRST SIGN OF CREAKING OR SWAYING, THE AXMAN QUICKLY STEPPED TO ONE SIDE AND STAYED PUT. A ROGUE BREEZE OR AN OFF CENTER TRUNK COULD LAND A "KICKBACK" IN THE WOODSMAN'S LAP.

THE NEXT THREE BLOWS WERE LEVELED DOWNWARD ON A FORTY-FIVE DEGREE ANGLE TO THE HORIZONTAL CUTS. THE DISTANCE BETWEEN THE TWO WAS ABOUT HALF THE TREE'S DIAMETER. AFTER THE FIRST CHUNK WAS FREED TO FORM THE HINGE, THE PROCESS WAS REPEATED TO MAKE A SMALLER "V," OPPOSITE AND 2 OR 3 INCHES ABOVE THE FIRST HINGE; THIS WOULD SEAL THE FATE OF THIS FUTURE POST OR BEAM. A SKILLED WOODCUTTER COULD SAVE TIME BY REMAINING ON THE SAME SIDE AND CHOPPING LEFT-HANDED.

RIP

AN ACCURATE SWING WITH A WEIGHTIER AX, THEN AS NOW, WILL BRING DOWN A TREE FASTER AND MORE EFFICIENTLY THAN MUSCLE POWER. A BUNCH OF STUMPS THAT RESEMBLED THE GNAWING OF BEAVERS WERE THE MONUMENTS LEFT BY ENTHUSIASTIC BUT INEXPERIENCED CHOPPERS. IT ALSO PAYS TO KNOW SOMETHING ABOUT THE CHARACTERISTICS OF WOOD BEFORE TAKING A TOOL TO IT. SINCE THE CELLULAR FIBERS THAT PIPE THE SAP UPWARD ARE PARALLEL TO THE TREE TRUNK, THEY RESIST A PERPENDICULAR CUT. RATHER THAN MASH THE FIBERS, AN EASIER AND SMOOTHER CUT CAN BE MADE WITH THE BLADE ANGLED INTO OR ALONG THE GRAIN.

7

TRIMMING

The felled tree was relieved of its branches by an ax blow from the bases toward the top.

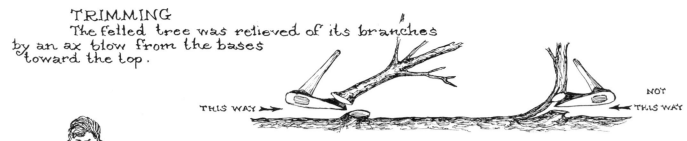

THIS WAY →

NOT ← THIS WAY

BUCKING

Each of the felled and trimmed trees had its specific place in the frame~work scheme. Each must be bucked or chopped to length. An additional several feet were allowed for any knots or imperfections that might interfere with a mortise or tenon.

The woodsman stood on the log with feet well apart unless he had some unwanted toes. The ax was held as with felling but the swing was downward. Twin angles were cut into the side of the log until a notch of forty~five degrees had reached the midpoint. Then the opposite side was attacked and a like notch made until the log was severed.

TOP VIEW

45°

45°

BARKING IRON (PEELING IRON, BARK SPUD)

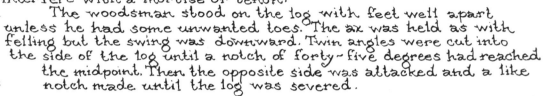

SHIELD-SHAPED BLADE

ROUND BLADE

SEMI~CIRCULAR BLADE

SPADE BLADE

The bark of a freshly cut log could be skinned with greater ease than that of a dried log. The barking iron, ranging up to 30 inches in length and pushed to yield bark strips, was either all iron or made with a wooden handle inserted into a socketed blade. There was a choice of iron~blade designs, but all were wedge~shaped on cross~section and slightly rounded on the top to better chisel off the bark.

The center of the debarked log was raised to knee height for a more convenient hewing. Two 4~foot lengths were chopped from the surplus wood to platform the log.

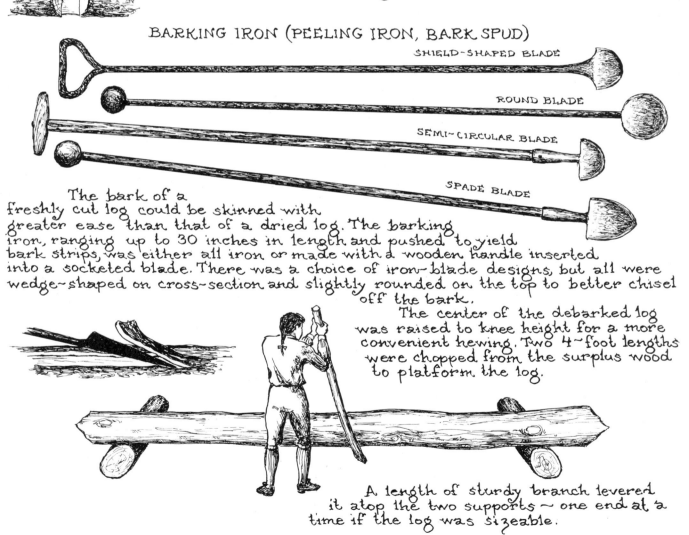

A length of sturdy branch levered it atop the two supports ~ one end at a time if the log was sizeable.

TIMBER DOGS

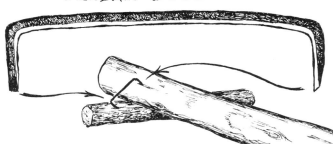

These large iron staples secured the log to be worked to the two smaller supporting logs. Depending on the diameter of the log, a dog could range from 6 to 18 inches in length.

The dog's teeth were either chisel~shaped parallel to the grain or were wrought into points. They were tapped into position with the ax poll.

CHALK LINE AND REEL

IF WHITTLED OF GREEN HICKORY OR ASH, THIS REEL BOW COULD BE BENT WITHOUT STEAMING.

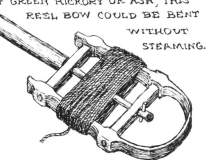

With the log skinned smooth and white and at an easier back~bending height, it was ready to be squared. To mark a straight guideline for hewing, a length of string was unwound from its reel. A chunk of chalk or a smut stick ~ a piece of charred wood from the fireplace ~ was rubbed into the string's fibers. The hewer cut a small nick at both ends of the log. With one end of the string secured in an end notch, the line was pulled taut and drawn into the opposite nick. At the middle of the log, the impregnated string was raised between the thumb and forefinger and released smartly.

WILLOW SMUT STICK (CHARCOAL FROM OTHER WOODS WAS TOO HARD FOR RUBBING)

WHITE CHALK (BLUE CHALK WAS OF A LATER CENTURY)

AN END NOTCH WAS ENOUGH TO HOLD THE STRING SECURELY.

SOMETIMES A SPLINTER WAS TAPPED INTO THE NOTCH FOR A TIE.

SNAPPING THE LINE

TOP VIEW OF LOG

BOTH SIDES OF THE LOG WERE SNAPPED BEFORE BEGINNING THE SQUARING.

FROM ROUND LOGS TO SQUARE

It wasn't time to retire the felling ax. Its one last contribution to the homestead framework was the scoring cuts to be made outside both chalk lines. The axman stood on the log as he did when bucking, used the same swing and angled cut to bite through the wood fibers. No chips were removed~ only a series of inch-deep slashes were made. Then the broadax would slice off the unwanted chunks between the scoring cuts. Chances are that more must be removed before "hewing to the line." Once again the ax cut into the partially flattened sides ~ perhaps two to four cuts every 6 inches or so that would penetrate to the chalk line and the excess wood beyond it. Those final score marks, made centuries earlier, are obvious today in America's enduring colonial buildings.

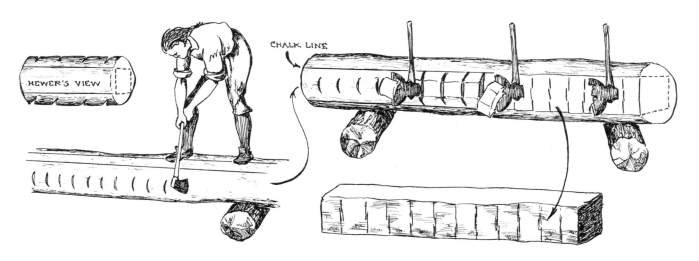

HEWER'S VIEW

CHALK LINE

THE BROADAX

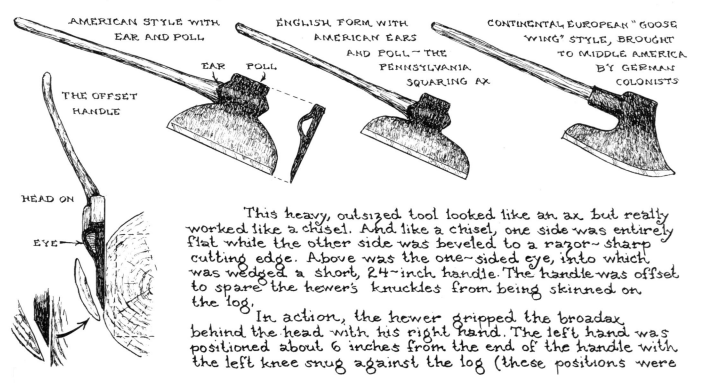

AMERICAN STYLE WITH EAR AND POLL

THE OFFSET HANDLE

EAR   POLL

ENGLISH FORM WITH AMERICAN EARS AND POLL ~ THE PENNSYLVANIA SQUARING AX

CONTINENTAL EUROPEAN "GOOSE WING" STYLE, BROUGHT TO MIDDLE AMERICA BY GERMAN COLONISTS

HEAD ON

EYE →

This heavy, outsized tool looked like an ax but really worked like a chisel. And like a chisel, one side was entirely flat while the other side was beveled to a razor~sharp cutting edge. Above was the one~sided eye, into which was wedged a short, 24~inch handle. The handle was offset to spare the hewer's knuckles from being skinned on the log.

In action, the hewer gripped the broadax behind the head with his right hand. The left hand was positioned about 6 inches from the end of the handle with the left knee snug against the log (these positions were reversed for left-handers). The broadax was raised about 6 inches above, and its flat side next to, the log. The cutting edge was pushed downward rather than being swung, to let the weight of the tool provide the muscle. As the hewer moved backward, he sliced off the chunks between the scoring cuts while keeping the worked side straight and true to the chalked line. The opposite side was then hewn parallel to the first.

THE SQUARE

THE CARPENTER'S SQUARE WAS A RUGGED WROUGHT-IRON "L" THAT COULD STAND UP UNDER HEAVY USAGE. IN ADDITION TO SQUARING LARGE TIMBER, IT WAS MARKED IN INCHES AND FEET FOR MEASURING. ALTHOUGH AVERAGING A 2-FOOT BLADE AND A 14-TO-18-INCH TONGUE, AS SHOWN HERE, THERE WERE SOME GIANTS WITH BLADES OF UP TO 8 FEET IN LENGTH.

THE TRY SQUARE WAS ESPECIALLY USEFUL WHEN SQUARING THE-POST-AND-BEAM JOINTS AND FOR FURNITURE MAKING. ALTHOUGH USUALLY OF A FINE HARDWOOD, AS MAHOGANY OR CHERRY, SOME HAD A WROUGHT-IRON BLADE. THE THICKER HANDLE WAS USED AS A FENCE, PRESSED AGAINST THE WORK. THE THINNER BLADE, UP TO 18 INCHES IN LENGTH, RESTED AGAINST THE SURFACE TO BE MARKED.

THIS WAS THE TOOL THAT KEPT THE WORK "ON THE SQUARE." THE TRY SQUARE AND ITS BIG BROTHER, THE CARPENTER'S SQUARE, WERE GUARANTEES THAT THE POST AND BEAM WOULD BE TRIMMED AND WOULD JOIN EACH OTHER AT AN ACCURATE NINETY DEGREES. HERE, TO BACK UP THE HEWER'S PRACTICED EYE, THE TWO REMAINING SIDES TO BE FLATTENED COULD BE SQUARE-CHECKED WITH THE TWO FINISHED FACES.

With two parallel faces hewn, the timber was rolled until it rested on one of them. No need for a timber dog here—the work would stay put when resting on its flat surface. Two parallel chalk lines were again snapped, the distance between being the same as between the two finished sides. Once again the felling ax scored the unwanted wood, and again the broadax sliced off the chunks between the scored marks. The squared post or beam was rough-hewn into shape, and that was good enough—unless the timber would be exposed in the homestead. Perhaps, too, there were a few humps left from the hewing that wanted skinning. Then it was a job for the adz— another tool that resembled the ax but was really a long-handled chisel that could smooth any wooden face to perfection.

CARPENTER'S FOOT ADZ

Like the broad ax, the sharp, straight cutting edge of the adz was beveled toward the handle. Its curved blade followed the arc as it was swung down to slice the wood fibers into thin sheets. The straight handle of colonial days, upward to 30 inches in length, was hafted perpendicular to the blade's faces. At that point the handle flared to better snug into the large, tapered eye socket. It was a clever bit of designing, for the handle could be backed through the underface to better sharpen the cutting edge. Reinserted, it wedged securely into the eye of the adz with every swing of the tool.

INSERTING THE HANDLE

To shave down a hewn surface, the adzman stood atop the timber, his back about 2 feet from one end. With an easy 12-inch-long swing, he sliced off a thin sheet just under his left shoe. A keen eye saved many a visit to the cobbler ~ or surgeon, for that matter. Moving forward, letting the weight of the adz do the flat chiseling, the adzman freed more slices until the surface was as smooth as a millpond. He then faced the end where he had begun and cleaned off the small section that remained.

ADZING THE HEWN LOG

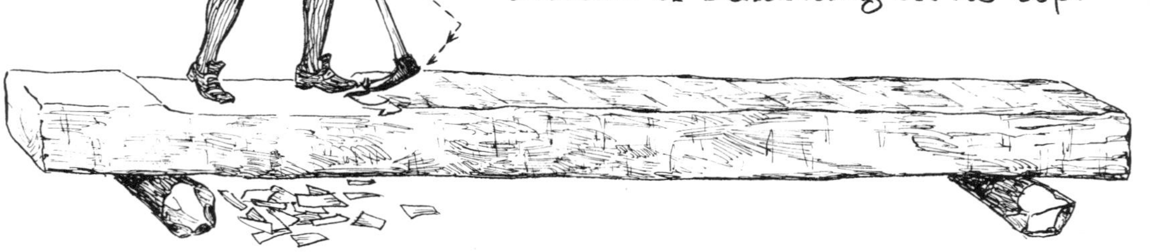

Sometimes the smaller poles for rafters or floor joists were flattened only on their upper surface. The remainder of the timber was left in the round. Without benefit of scoring cuts, the adz could level the top in jigtime. Since these were from smaller diameter trees, it was frequently easier to straddle the log instead of balancing on its top.

TIMBER CARRIER

Now that the logs had been square~hewed, freed of unwanted wood and perhaps tidied up with the adz, there was the matter of hauling their considerable numbers off to the building site (the scattering of chips and trimmed branches that lay on the forest floor would disintegrate and disappear, replaced by new seedlings.) The common skidding sleds or the two~wheeled cart just wouldn't do. The fresh timbers were smooth and clean, and no right~thinking colonial carpenter would employ his mortise-and-tenon tools on wood encrusted with mud and sand. The log-draggers shown here were useful only for moving raw logs for short distances.

LOGGING SLEDS

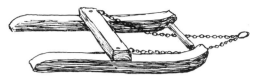

THE GO-DEVIL SLED DRAGGED LOGS USING ONE HORSE OR OX.

THE LARGE AND HEAVIER YARDING SLED COULD PULL FIVE LOGS WITH TWO ANIMALS.

The snow blankets that covered the more northerly colonies made the logging sled a natural. Even in the warm months or in the snow-free southern areas, the runners slid reasonably well over the forest floor. These sleds were for short hauls between the felling site and the skidway—the nearby collection "yard."

The forward end of each unworked "log" was chained to the crosspiece spanning the runners. The back ends were dragged behind—and that just wouldn't do for any freshly square-hewn timber. Any ground-in mud, sand, or like debris would not be looked on kindly when the mortise-and-tenon work began.

TRACE CHAINS TO HORSES' HARNESSES

THE TWO-SLED

Here was the answer to the problem. It made sense to combine the go-devil and the yarding sled into a two-sled. A small version of about 4 feet in width could be snaked around the trees with a pair of horses or oxen. The low rig made for easy loading of the hewn timber from its log supports, and, once on the two-sled, the future post or beam never touched the ground.

WHEELED CARTS AND WAGONS

THIS HIGH-WHEELED CART WAS BACKED OVER THE FRONT OF THE LOG ① AND THE TONGUE RAISED VERTICALLY WITH A POLE. ② GRAPPLING TONGS, SUSPENDED FROM THE HUGE AXLE, WERE THEREBY LOWERED ON AND THEN SECURED TO THE LOG. THE TEAM THEN PULLED THE TONGUE TO THE HORIZONTAL, AND THE LOG WAS LIFTED FOR DRAGGING.

THE TONGUE WAS 12 TO 16 FEET.

13

Like the go-devil and the yard sleds the log cart was useful for dragging raw logs, not clean, freshly hewn timber from the forest. They saw service in the snow-free south or wherever the land surface was firm and level or gently rolling. Any abrupt decline made holding the load back a difficult chore and might mean a runaway cart.

HAULING TO THE SITE

Colonial records make little or no mention about the loading of timber at the assembly or skidway "yard." Therefore the last hitch in the haul to the building site with the two-sled or the timber wagon is conjectural but probably went like this:

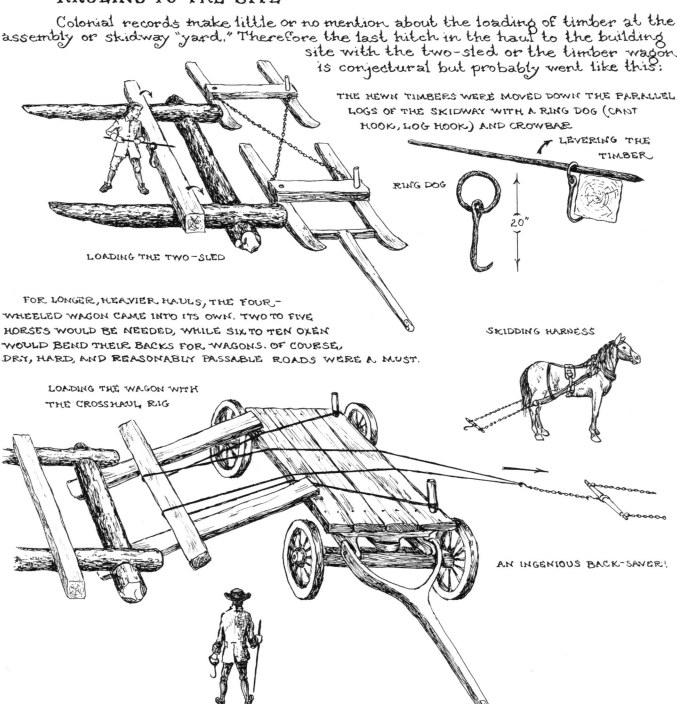

THE HEWN TIMBERS WERE MOVED DOWN THE PARALLEL LOGS OF THE SKIDWAY WITH A RING DOG (CANT HOOK, LOG HOOK) AND CROWBAR

LEVERING THE TIMBER

RING DOG

20"

LOADING THE TWO-SLED

FOR LONGER, HEAVIER HAULS, THE FOUR-WHEELED WAGON CAME INTO ITS OWN. TWO TO FIVE HORSES WOULD BE NEEDED, WHILE SIX TO TEN OXEN WOULD BEND THEIR BACKS FOR WAGONS. OF COURSE, DRY, HARD, AND REASONABLY PASSABLE ROADS WERE A MUST.

SKIDDING HARNESS

LOADING THE WAGON WITH THE CROSSHAUL RIG

AN INGENIOUS BACK-SAVER!

14

HORSES OR OXEN?

The secret to hauling heavy timber was a slow and steady pace, and for this oxen had no equal. Horses were certainly more agile and faster but also tired sooner. Being more high-strung, they could be skitterish when the going was difficult. They had to be draped in a relatively costly harness. Somewhat finicky appetites called for feed three times daily. Not so with the oxen, for they were docile, even-tempered, and certainly strong enough to plod up steep slopes with little effort. (A castrated bull, facing hard labor as an ox, might be little cheered by his newfound qualities.) Their large hooves could take the wagon through muck and mire where horses would soon bog down. Oxen were satisfied with a single meal of coarse feed and their yoke harness was easily shaped from the wood at hand. Further, only one teamster need manage a team of eight to ten oxen, while no more than four or five horses could be worked by one person. It was little wonder that the colonists held a high regard for these great lumbering beasts.

SEASONING THE WOOD

Once the hewn timber had arrived at the building site, it was stacked in a shady spot, each separated by thin wooden strips. Slow, uniform drying was a must. Since up to two-thirds of the weight of fresh wood is water, the swollen cells cut with far greater ease when green than after losing their moisture. Doubters should try splitting a few chunks of firewood that are green, then a few that are seasoned. A freshly cut piece will slice open like a ripe pumpkin, while a dried one will often fight back. Only when that wood has lost about five-sixths of the water by weight will it be strong and stiff enough to support its part of the framing. The rule of thumb, then, was to work the timber when green and put it to use when dried.

CHECKS AND CRACKS FROM TOO RAPID DRYING

STACKED FOR SLOW AIR DRYING

Annual growth rings shrink during the drying process. Those closest to the outer surface will contract before those nearer the center, if the sun or warm weather are excessive. As the moisture evaporates and the outer rings pull apart, checks and cracks result. Hopefully, slow drying after the winter felling will allow easy cutting of the mortises and tenons without much checking.

MORTISE   TENON

SHOULDER

Since each mortise hole would shrink slightly with seasoning, it was worthwhile to make the tenon slightly shorter to prevent its being pushed out. The builder would also be well advised to cut a supporting shoulder to foresee any shortening of the horizontal beam and its tenons as it dried.

Before the cutting of the mortises and tenons could begin, each timber must have a final checking for problem spots such as knots, checks and splits, insect damage, or any grain that wandered badly from the horizontal. After plotting the best placement for the connecting joints, the timber was sawed to the final length.

15

CUTTING TIMBER TO SIZE

THE SAWING HORSE

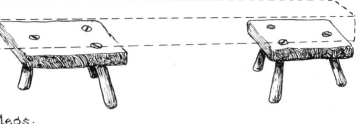

To bring the timber up to a workable height, two sawing stools were used to raise the work up to the carpenter's knees. Each pair had sturdy tops of about 3 feet in length that were supported by three or four legs.

Another version was the sawing dogs for heavy, lengthy timbers. Each 7-foot plank was raised at one end by splayed legs. The timber was levered to the desired height and pegs inserted into one of the plank holes to secure the work in place.

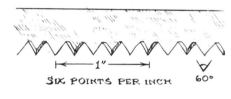

CARPENTER'S SAW (FRAMED-BOW CROSSCUT SAW)

To cut the hewn timber into proper framing lengths, the rugged inflexible blade of the framed-bow crosscut saw was the saw of choice. The business edge was a series of teeth or cutters. They were crosscut teeth, designed to slice across the wood fibers. Five to eleven points to the inch were usual. The coarser the work and the softer the wood, the fewer points per inch were necessary.

|← 1" →|

SIX POINTS PER INCH   60°

CARPENTER'S SAW

TENSION CORD AND TURNBUCKLE

STRETCHER

CHEEK

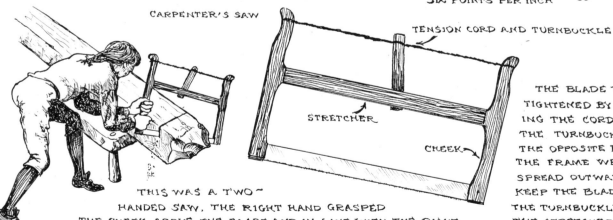

THE BLADE WAS TIGHTENED BY TWISTING THE CORD WITH THE TURNBUCKLE. THE OPPOSITE ENDS OF THE FRAME WERE SPREAD OUTWARD KEEP THE BLADE TAUT. THE TURNBUCKLE AGAINST THE STRETCHER PREVENTED ANY UNWINDING OF THE CORD.

THIS WAS A TWO-HANDED SAW. THE RIGHT HAND GRASPED THE CHEEK ABOVE THE BLADE AND IN LINE WITH THE RIGHT SHOULDER. THE CUT WAS BEGUN ON A LINE MARKED WITH A SQUARE ON THE TOP AND THE FRONT OF THE TIMBER. THE BLADE WAS PULLED BACK GENTLY UNTIL THE CUT WAS BEGUN, THEN PUSHED TO THE FINISH WITH RHYTHMIC STROKES.

IN LATER YEARS, THIS WAS KNOWN AS A BUCKSAW FOR BUCKING~ CUTTING A LOG INTO LENGTHS.

SAW SET

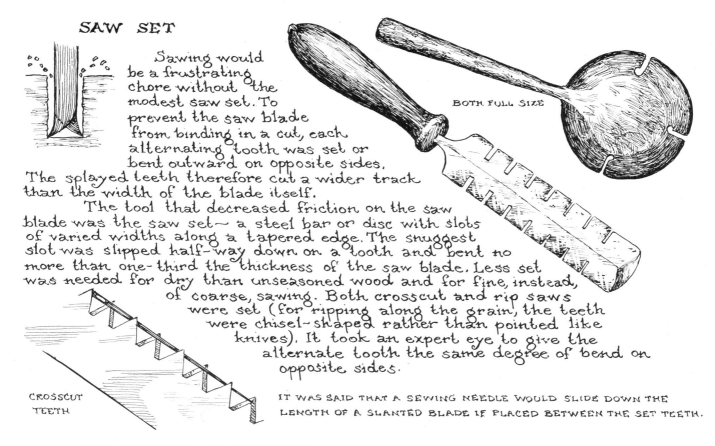

Sawing would be a frustrating chore without the modest saw set. To prevent the saw blade from binding in a cut, each alternating tooth was set or bent outward on opposite sides. The splayed teeth therefore cut a wider track than the width of the blade itself.

The tool that decreased friction on the saw blade was the saw set— a steel bar or disc with slots of varied widths along a tapered edge. The snuggest slot was slipped half-way down on a tooth and bent no more than one-third the thickness of the saw blade. Less set was needed for dry than unseasoned wood and for fine, instead, of coarse, sawing. Both crosscut and rip saws were set (for ripping along the grain, the teeth were chisel-shaped rather than pointed like knives). It took an expert eye to give the alternate tooth the same degree of bend on opposite sides.

BOTH FULL SIZE

CROSSCUT TEETH

IT WAS SAID THAT A SEWING NEEDLE WOULD SLIDE DOWN THE LENGTH OF A SLANTED BLADE IF PLACED BETWEEN THE SET TEETH.

SCRIBING THE JOINTS

When two or more timbers were locked together, a joint was formed. Properly done, each joint was as though the living trees had grown together to form a strong and enduring house frame. Joinery was reserved for the seasoned, wood-wise craftsman who took a real pride in his skills. The hurried and often slapdash stud-and-plywood constructions of today would have no place in his scheme of building. That included the permanent joining of more than two hundred massive timbers in the average colonial home. With twice that number of joints.

Matching gauge markings ruled off the variety of joinings, and the most usual of these were the mortise-and-tenon joints. To prevent weakening of the posts and beams, the width of each mortise slot and its insertion tenon was generally between a third and a half the width of the timber.

MORTISING GAUGE

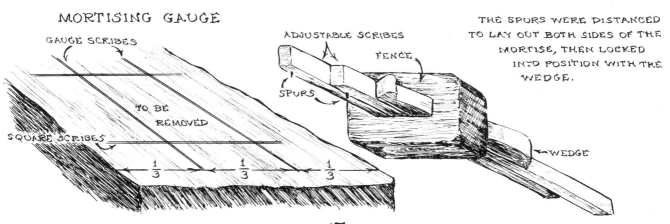

THE SPURS WERE DISTANCED TO LAY OUT BOTH SIDES OF THE MORTISE, THEN LOCKED INTO POSITION WITH THE WEDGE.

GAUGE SCRIBES

TO BE REMOVED

SQUARE SCRIBES

$\frac{1}{3}$ $\frac{1}{3}$ $\frac{1}{3}$

ADJUSTABLE SCRIBES

FENCE

SPURS

WEDGE

MARKING GAUGE

Here the marking gauge scribes out the tenon projection. Because the hewn surface of the timber was not mill-pond smooth, a longer fence rode over any irregularities.

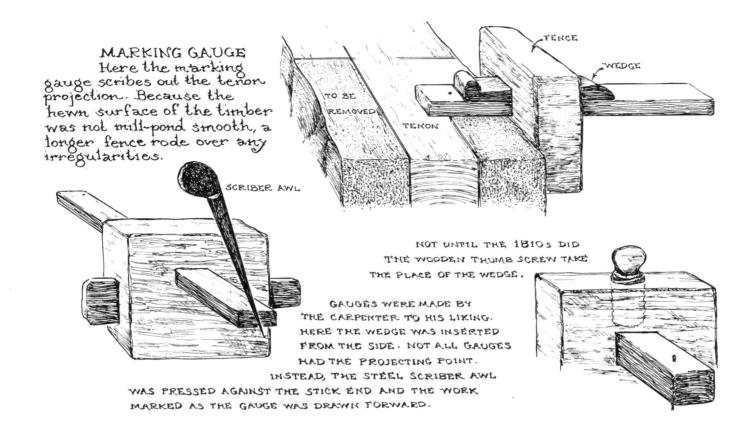

FENCE

WEDGE

TO BE REMOVED

TENON

SCRIBER AWL

NOT UNTIL THE 1810s DID THE WOODEN THUMB SCREW TAKE THE PLACE OF THE WEDGE.

GAUGES WERE MADE BY THE CARPENTER TO HIS LIKING. HERE THE WEDGE WAS INSERTED FROM THE SIDE. NOT ALL GAUGES HAD THE PROJECTING POINT. INSTEAD, THE STEEL SCRIBER AWL WAS PRESSED AGAINST THE STICK END AND THE WORK MARKED AS THE GAUGE WAS DRAWN FORWARD.

TIMBER SCRIBE (RACE KNIFE)

Each tenon must fit precisely into its own mortise. To be certain that each joint would be a marriage of the proper partners, every matched pair must be marked with the same number. The timber scribe could cut these numbers to a depth that would remain crisp and clear until the timbers were joined.

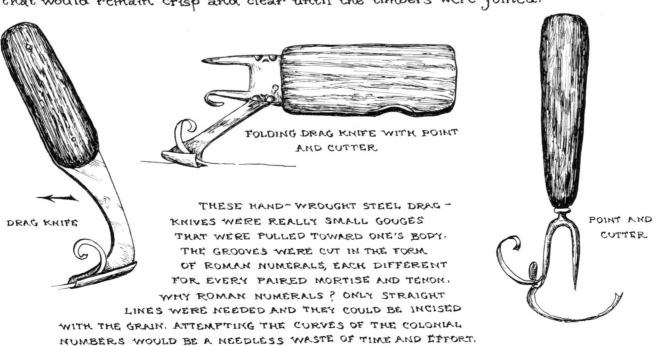

FOLDING DRAG KNIFE WITH POINT AND CUTTER

DRAG KNIFE

THESE HAND-WROUGHT STEEL DRAG-KNIVES WERE REALLY SMALL GOUGES THAT WERE PULLED TOWARD ONE'S BODY. THE GROOVES WERE CUT IN THE FORM OF ROMAN NUMERALS, EACH DIFFERENT FOR EVERY PAIRED MORTISE AND TENON. WHY ROMAN NUMERALS? ONLY STRAIGHT LINES WERE NEEDED AND THEY COULD BE INCISED WITH THE GRAIN. ATTEMPTING THE CURVES OF THE COLONIAL NUMBERS WOULD BE A NEEDLESS WASTE OF TIME AND EFFORT.

POINT AND CUTTER

THE COMPASS POINT AND CUTTER GOUGE
PRODUCED CURVES AND CIRCLES FOR CODE
MARKS TO SHOW THE PLACEMENT OF EACH
TIMBER IN THE FRAMEWORK SCHEME.

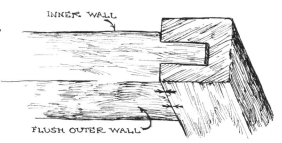

TRICKS OF THE TRADE

The outside faces of the completed framework must be flush to receive the exterior wall boards. Since hewn posts were not usually of the same cross-sectional size as the beam to be joined, centering a mortise and tenon would not give a continuous outside plane. Therefore the old timers scribed their measured gauge markings from the timber side that would face outward from the framework.

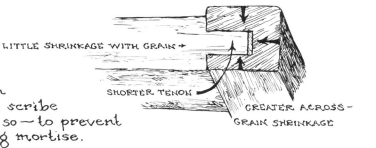

INNER WALL

FLUSH OUTER WALL

The colonial carpenter was mindful of the shrinkage of his timber that was still in the process of seasoning. As it continued to dry, the mortise hole would contract across the grain. The tenon would lose little length with the grain from lost moisture. It was prudent to scribe the tenon a bit shorter~ say $\frac{1}{8}$ inch or so ~to prevent its being pushed out of the shortening mortise.

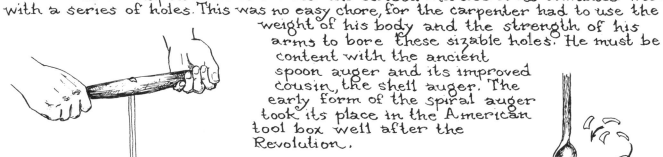

LITTLE SHRINKAGE WITH GRAIN →

SHORTER TENON

GREATER ACROSS-GRAIN SHRINKAGE

SHAPING THE TIMBER MORTISE

AUGERS

This T-shaped drill could rid the scribed mortise of its unwanted wood with a series of holes. This was no easy chore, for the carpenter had to use the weight of his body and the strength of his arms to bore these sizable holes. He must be content with the ancient spoon auger and its improved cousin, the shell auger. The early form of the spiral auger took its place in the American tool box well after the Revolution.

NOT UNTIL 1770 DID ENGLAND'S PHINEAS COOK INVENT THE EFFICIENT SHAVING-REMOVING SPIRAL AUGER.

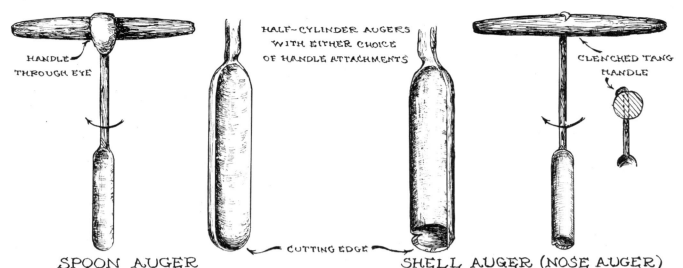

HANDLE
THROUGH EYE

HALF-CYLINDER AUGERS
WITH EITHER CHOICE
OF HANDLE ATTACHMENTS

CLENCHED TANG
HANDLE

CUTTING EDGE

SPOON AUGER

THE BUSINESS END OF THE SPOON WAS A
SHARP, ROUNDED EDGE THAT CUT MUCH LIKE
A ROTATING GOUGE. A SMALLER HALF-
INCH-DEPTH STARTING HOLE WAS HELPFUL
BEFORE BORING. AFTER THREE OR FOUR
TURNS, THE BIT WAS REMOVED TO SPOON
OUT THE SHAVINGS.

SHELL AUGER (NOSE AUGER)

POPULAR SINCE THE SEVENTEENTH CENTURY, THE
HALF-CYLINDER BLADE HAD A SHELF-LIKE CUTTER
AT ITS "NOSE." BEFORE DRILLING, THE SURFACE OF
THE WOOD HAD TO BE SCOOPED WITH A GOUGE. THE
DOWNWARD SLANT OF CUTTER COULD THEN BITE INTO
THE WOOD FIBERS. AS WITH THE SPOON AUGER, THE
BIT MUST BE REMOVED OFTEN, CARRYING OUT THE
SHAVINGS ON ITS CUTTER SHELF.

CHISELS

The auger's roughly-formed mortise with its slightly overlapping holes was
ready to be pared down to the scribed outline. Enter the chisel family, the last word
in finishing the joints square and true. A snug joining was the sign of a true
craftsman, not the weekend handyman.

THE FIRMER OR FORMING CHISEL

From the French "fermoir" meaning "to form," this all-purpose chisel lived up
to its name. The parallel blade was sturdily wrought for use with a mallet, cutting
a width of wood from $\frac{1}{16}$ to 3 inches wide. Some blades had beveled edges to
better clean out corners such as on mortise work. Most firmers had a long
extension, that was embedded in the wooden handle.

THIS EXAMPLE HAS THE
BEVELED SIDES FOR
CLEARING EDGES.

THE FRAMING CHISEL (AMERICAN CHISEL)

Here was the chisel for heavy going. The long and strong parallel-edged
blade ranged between 2 to $4\frac{1}{2}$ inches in width. Generally, the wooden handle
was well-socketed instead of having a blade tang. Overall length was about $1\frac{1}{2}$
feet.

JOINER'S MORTISING CHISEL

The rugged blade was unusually thick to permit the levering out of deep shavings from the mortise ends. Equally sturdy was the tanged oval handle on cross-section that could withstand heavy mallet blows.

CORNER CHISEL

The ninety-degree cutting edge squared out deep mortise corners with greater ease than either the firmer or the mortise chisel. It was socketed with a wooden handle or was entirely wrought of steel for use with the mallet.

SLICK

This outsized chisel lived up to its name. Its 3- to 4-inch-wide blade could slick off sheets of wood as easily as paring off the skin of a crisp apple. The length (up to 30 inches), weight, and sharpness gave great control when pushed with the hands and shoulders. A mallet was never used.

MALLETS

Mallets were wooden hammers. If any wooden-handled tool such as a chisel was in want of pounding, the mallet was a must. A metal hammer wouldn't do because it would soon split a wood handle or make its end mushroomlike. Wood against wood was, and still is, the rule. Throughout the joining of the frame timbers, large mallets (commanders) drove the joints together, then a smaller mallet struck home the treenails (trunnels) to lock them for all time.

CYLINDRICAL-HEAD MALLET

Every chisel deserved its own mallet—and the colonial joiner could have any number without being out of pocket a farthing. All it took was a straight limb of hickory, beech, ash, hornbeam, dogwood, or some such close-grained hardwood. While the wood was still green, a hole was bored for a seasoned handle of hickory or ash. As the head dried and

THE SLICK

21

shrank, the handle was forever locked in place.

CARPENTER'S AND JOINER'S MALLET

This was a heavy tool for heavy joining work. As with the cylindrical head mallet, it was made of similar, close-grained hardwoods. Its shape was distinctive, for both sides were flat while the remaining sides were often curved much like a wagon-wheel section. The shape followed a similar arc on the swing down to the chisel handle.

Often the handle was wedged in from the outer curve and remained tightly in place from the centrifugal force of the swing.

MORTISING TOOLS IN ACTION

FIRMER OR FRAMING CHISEL

1.

THE MORTISE OUTLINE WAS SCORED LIGHTLY TO PREVENT THE AUGER FROM SLIVERING INTO THE SURROUNDING WOOD.

SHELL AUGER

2.

A LINE OF OVERLAPPING AUGER HOLES OF NEARLY THE SAME DIAMETER AS THE MORTISE WIDTH

FIRMER, FRAMING OR MORTISE CHISEL

3.

THE EXCESS WOOD WAS GRADUALLY REMOVED BY CHISELING INWARD FROM THE SIDES AND ENDS, BEVELED EDGE DOWN. THE STURDY BLADE OF THE MORTISE CHISEL WAS HELPFUL TO LEVER THE CHIPS OUT.

4. VERTICAL CUTS ALONG THE SCORED LINE WERE NOT MADE INITIALLY. PRESSURE OF THE WOOD AGAINST THE BEVELED CUTTING EDGE WOULD FORCE THE FLAT FACE OF THE CHISEL ON AN OUTWARD ANGLE.

CORNER CHISEL

5.

AFTER THE WASTE WOOD WAS CHISELED FREE, THE CORNER CHISEL, IF HELD VERTICALLY, WOULD MAKE PERFECTLY SQUARE ENDS.

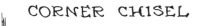

6.

WITH THE SIDES AND ENDS CHISELED FAIRLY VERTICAL, THE FINAL SHAVING OF THE REMAINING WOOD COULD BEGIN. ALTHOUGH THE FIRMER AND FRAMING CHISELS COULD BE USED, THE SLICK COULD MAKE AN ADMIRABLY SMOOTH AND PRECISE JOB OF FINISHING THE INNER MORTISE FACES.

A PERIODIC CHECK WITH THE TRY SQUARE WAS A MUST.

SHOULDER MORTISE

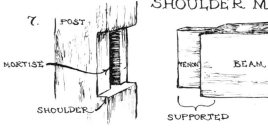

7.

POST

MORTISE

SHOULDER

TENON   BEAM

SUPPORTED

WEIGHT-BEARING POST MORTISES CALLED FOR A MOST IMPORTANT ADDITION—A SHOULDER, THAT WOULD GIVE ADDED SUPPORT TO HEAVY BEAMS. THE TENON SHOULDN'T CARRY THE LOAD ALONE.

THE SHOULDER WAS SCRIBED WITH THE SQUARE, CUT TO THE PROPER DEPTH WITH A CROSSCUT SAW, AND THE EXCESS WOOD CHISELED FREE.

SHAPING THE TENON

TENON MARKED $\frac{1}{8}$ INCH SHORTER THAN MORTISE DEPTH (SEE PAGE 19).

1.

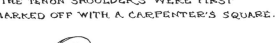

THE TENON SHOULDERS WERE FIRST MARKED OFF WITH A CARPENTER'S SQUARE.

2.

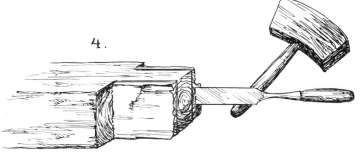

INTERIOR SURFACE

OUTER SURFACE

THE MARKING GAUGE (SEE PAGE 18) SCRIBED THE TENON FROM THE EXTERIOR FACE OF THE TIMBER. THE COMPLETED FRAMEWORK WOULD THEN BE FLUSH FOR THE SHEATHING (PAGE 19).

3.

SHOULDER

CROSSCUTTING THE SHOULDERS

4.

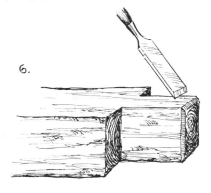

THE FRAMING CHISEL SPLIT OFF CHUNKS OF WOOD WHILE NOT CROWDING THE SCRIBED TENON OUTLINE.

5.

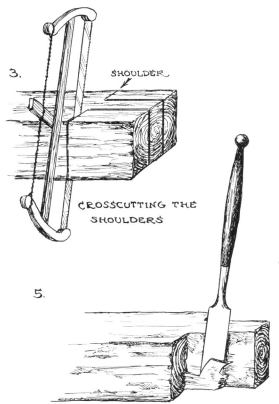

THE SLICK GAVE A FINAL SMOOTHING AND SQUARING ON THE TENON FACE WITH THE HELP OF THE TRY SQUARE.

6.

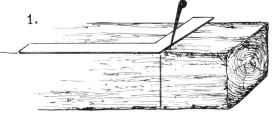

FOR AN EASIER INSERTION OF THE TENON INTO THE MORTISE, THE SLICK CHAMFERED THE FORWARD EDGES.

23

PEGGING THE JOINT

One might assume that after the tenon had been driven into the mortise, the peg holes were drilled. Not so. To really snug any joint as tightly as possible, the peg holes were offset by drawboring between $\frac{1}{8}$ and $\frac{1}{4}$ inch. Later, when the peg was driven home, the tenon would be drawn to its full extent into the mortise.

DRAWING IN
THE TENON

TOP VIEW

THE COMMANDER

THIS HEAVY, KINGSIZED MALLET DROVE THE MORTISE-AND-TENON JOINT TOGETHER. THE MASSIVE TIMBERS WERE POSITIONED ON A FLAT SURFACE. IT WAS THE GREAT PERSUADER AMONG MALLETS.

DRIFT WEDGE (HOOK PIN)

Rather than risk a fractured pin in the drawing together of the joint, the drift wedge was an unbreakable but temporary substitute. The tapered iron or steel pin drew the mortise and tenon together as tightly as possible. Then, its job done, it was pried or hammered out, using the end hook. The bored holes were more in line, although still slightly offset. It was time for the actual pegging.

← A FEW BLOWS REMOVED THE DRIFT WEDGE FROM THE PEG HOLES.

TREENAILS

Pegs were the treenails (trunnels) that locked the joints together for keeps. The colonial builders must have been pleasured to secure their all-wooden framework together with all-wooden nails. Yankee make-do with the raw materials at hand was a part of that independent spirit that made the American Revolution inevitable.

THE FROE

Slabs of hardwood, an inch or more in thickness, were split off a foot-long block with the froe.

THE BLADE OF THIS L-SHAPED TOOL MIGHT RUN FROM 6 TO 24 INCHES IN LENGTH AND ABOUT 2 INCHES IN WIDTH. THE EYE, WROUGHT MUCH LIKE THE EARLY AXES, HELD AN 18-INCH HANDLE.

← A MUCH-USED MAUL SHOWED THE SCARS FROM PAST FROE BASHINGS.

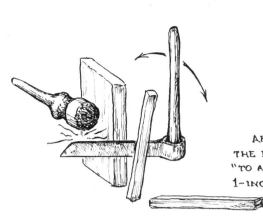

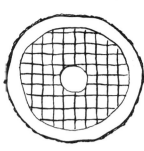

SAPWOOD PERISHED WHEN EXPOSED TO THE WEATHER.

STRAIGHT-GRAINED BOARD-WOOD MADE RUGGED PEGS.

HEARTWOOD WAS TOO BRITTLE FOR PEGS.

AFTER THE MALLET HAD DRIVEN THE BLADE INTO THE HARDWOOD, THE FROE HANDLE WAS USED AS A LEVER, PUSHING AND PULLING IT "TO AND FRO" TO WIDEN THE SPLIT. THIS WAS REPEATED UNTIL A 1-INCH SLAB PARTED COMPANY. EACH SLAB WAS THEN SPLIT INTO 1-INCH-SQUARE STICKS. SINCE EACH STICK WAS MADE UP OF PARALLEL FIBERS, STRAIGHT AND STRONG, THEY MADE ADMIRABLE JOINT NAILS.

"Square pegs in round holes," as the saying goes, "make a poor fit." An octagonal-sided peg, on the other hand, had its corners just flattened enough to give an added tightness when driven in. Further, if the peg were tapered at an end, it could pass through the offset mortise-and-tenon holes. The draw knife and the shaving horse teamed up to shape the peg to its proper form.

THE DRAW KNIFE

The long, chisel-like blade ended in two curved tangs that were clenched over turned wooden handles. This versatile roughing-out tool was pulled toward the body, beveled cutting edge either up or down according to one's preference. When trimming an inner curve, however, the beveled edge would face downward.

ALSO KNOWN AS THE DRAW SHAVE

FLAT, SLIGHTLY CURVED BLADE

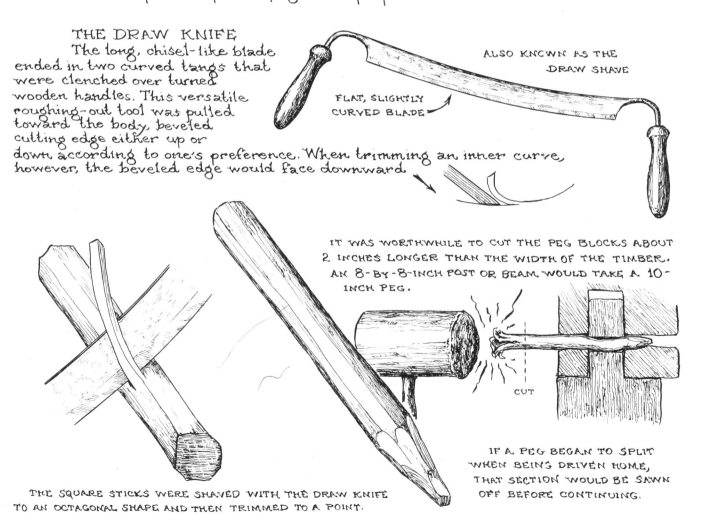

IT WAS WORTHWHILE TO CUT THE PEG BLOCKS ABOUT 2 INCHES LONGER THAN THE WIDTH OF THE TIMBER. AN 8-BY-8-INCH POST OR BEAM WOULD TAKE A 10-INCH PEG.

CUT

IF A PEG BEGAN TO SPLIT WHEN BEING DRIVEN HOME, THAT SECTION WOULD BE SAWN OFF BEFORE CONTINUING.

THE SQUARE STICKS WERE SHAVED WITH THE DRAW KNIFE TO AN OCTAGONAL SHAPE AND THEN TRIMMED TO A POINT.

25

THE SHAVING HORSE

To shave those square pegs to better fit a round hole, the shaving horse was a must. This outsized clamp, a contant companion to the draw knife, was just as helpful when roughing out shingles, clapboards, and furniture; trimming the wood before it was turned on the lathe; and shaping bowls and utensils, tool handles, poles, fences, carvings, sculptures and the like. Often such projects would be finished by firelight during the winter months.

"Little shavers" and older folk took their turns on the shaving horse.

Its workings were simple. Foot pressure against the foot rest ① forced the dumbhead clamp ② forward to hold the work. Sometimes a springy hickory branch ③ was secured into the end of the ramp ④. The worksaver snapped the clamp back to an open position when the foot was released. If you have a draw knife that's gathering dust, give thought to making your own horse. This colonial original was sketched at the Hadley Farm Museum at Hadley, Massachusetts.

TWINE

BENCH

NOTE THAT THE RAMP SHOULD BE IN LINE WITH THE ELBOWS.

1. The Bench   O = DRILL   ------ = SAW

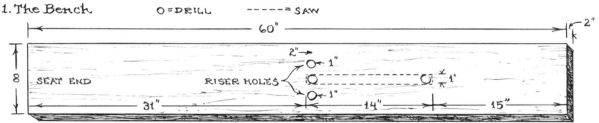

60"   2"

8"   SEAT END   RISER HOLES   2"   1"   x 1"

31"   14"   15"

THE PLANK IS 2" x 8" x 60" AND OF WHITE OAK.   DRILL THE 1-INCH HOLES AS SHOWN, AND SAW OUT THE DOTTED SLOT.

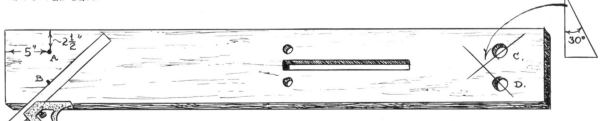

5"   ~2½"   A   B   C.   D.   30°

FOR THE LEG HOLES, MEASURE IN FROM EACH CORNER AS AT "A"; SCRIBE A FORTY-FIVE-DEGREE ANGLE AT EACH CORNER AS AT "B." CUT A CARDBOARD THIRTY-DEGREE ANGLE AND LINE UP WITH THE SCRIBED LINES. WITH A 1½-INCH BIT, BORE THE FOUR HOLES USING THE CARDBOARD ANGLE GUIDE. THE LEGS WILL HAVE THE SAME SPLAY.

BEVEL SEAT EDGES

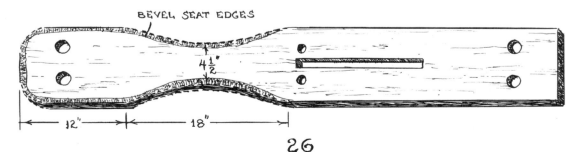

4½"

12"   18"

26

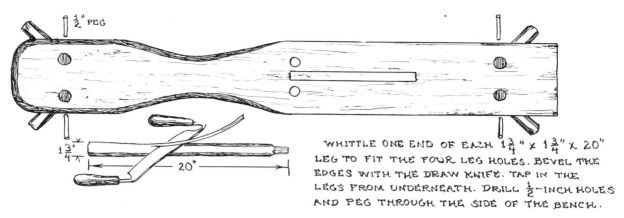

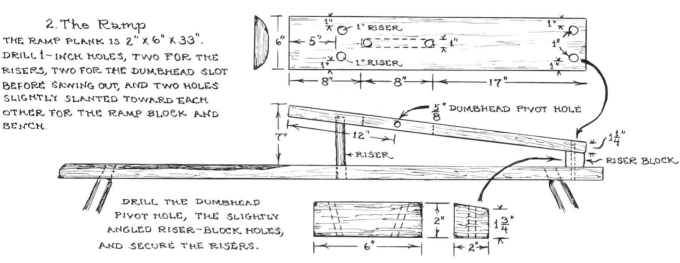

½" PEG

1¾"

20"

WHITTLE ONE END OF EACH 1¾" x 1¾" x 20" LEG TO FIT THE FOUR LEG HOLES. BEVEL THE EDGES WITH THE DRAW KNIFE. TAP IN THE LEGS FROM UNDERNEATH. DRILL ½-INCH HOLES AND PEG THROUGH THE SIDE OF THE BENCH.

2. The Ramp

THE RAMP PLANK IS 2" x 6" x 33". DRILL 1-INCH HOLES, TWO FOR THE RISERS, TWO FOR THE DUMBHEAD SLOT BEFORE SAWING OUT, AND TWO HOLES SLIGHTLY SLANTED TOWARD EACH OTHER FOR THE RAMP BLOCK AND BENCH.

6"   5"   ¼" 1" RISER   1" ¼
       1" ¼   ¼" 1"
       ¼" 1" RISER   1" ¼
8"   8"   17"

⅝" DUMBHEAD PIVOT HOLE
7"   12"   1¼"
RISER   RISER BLOCK

DRILL THE DUMBHEAD PIVOT HOLE, THE SLIGHTLY ANGLED RISER-BLOCK HOLES, AND SECURE THE RISERS.

2"   1¾"
6"   2"

3. THE DUMBHEAD ~ THE HARDWORKING CLAMP WITH THE STRANGE NAME

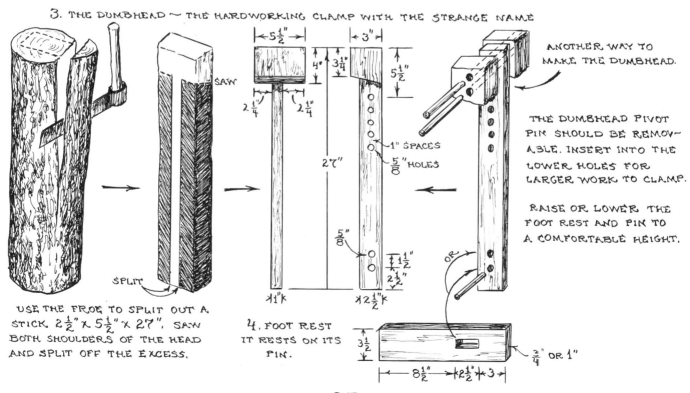

SAW

SPLIT

USE THE FROE TO SPLIT OUT A STICK 2½" x 5½" x 27". SAW BOTH SHOULDERS OF THE HEAD AND SPLIT OFF THE EXCESS.

5½"   3"
4"   3¼"   5½"
2¼"   2¼"
27"
1" SPACES
⅝" HOLES
⅝"
1½"
2½"
1"   2½"

4. FOOT REST IT RESTS ON ITS PIN.

ANOTHER WAY TO MAKE THE DUMBHEAD.

THE DUMBHEAD PIVOT PIN SHOULD BE REMOVABLE. INSERT INTO THE LOWER HOLES FOR LARGER WORK TO CLAMP.

RAISE OR LOWER THE FOOT REST AND PIN TO A COMFORTABLE HEIGHT.

OR

3½"
8½"   2½"   3
¾" OR 1"

27

THE FOUNDATION

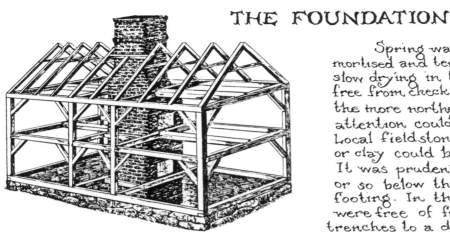

Spring was fast approaching. The mortised and tenoned timbers were stacked for slow drying in the still-cool weather~ hopefully free from checks. With the frozen ground in the more northerly colonies becoming workable, attention could be given to the foundation. Local fieldstones were there for the taking, or clay could be baked into brick blocks. It was prudent to lay their base a foot or so below the frost line for a heaveless footing. In those fortunate colonies that were free of freezing weather, digging trenches to a depth of two or so feet would give a firm foundation. Since many homes of the period could boast of a cellar, the whereabouts of the frost line was of little matter.

FOUNDATION SILLS

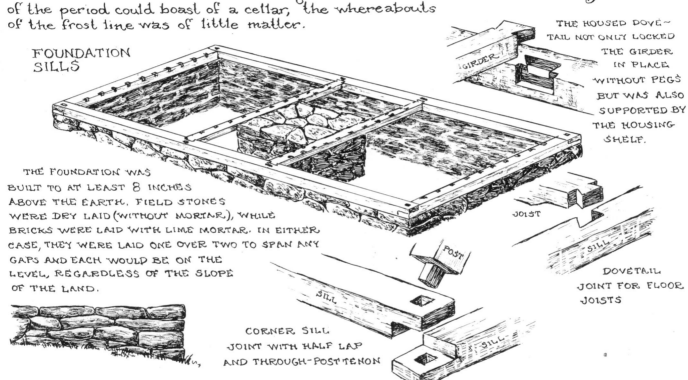

THE HOUSED DOVE~ TAIL NOT ONLY LOCKED THE GIRDER IN PLACE WITHOUT PEGS BUT WAS ALSO SUPPORTED BY THE HOUSING SHELF.

GIRDER

JOIST

THE FOUNDATION WAS BUILT TO AT LEAST 8 INCHES ABOVE THE EARTH. FIELD STONES WERE DRY LAID (WITHOUT MORTAR), WHILE BRICKS WERE LAID WITH LIME MORTAR. IN EITHER CASE, THEY WERE LAID ONE OVER TWO TO SPAN ANY GAPS AND EACH WOULD BE ON THE LEVEL, REGARDLESS OF THE SLOPE OF THE LAND.

SILL

DOVETAIL JOINT FOR FLOOR JOISTS

POST

SILL

CORNER SILL JOINT WITH HALF LAP AND THROUGH-POST TENON

SILL

SQUARING THE SILLS

The Greek philosopher Pythagoras passed down a theorem through the centuries, forgotten by many but not by those practical post-and-beam builders. Sills could be squared by measuring off units of a 3-4-5 triangle. A unit could be a tool handle or whatever.

THREE LENGTHS WERE MEASURED OFF ON A SILL AND FOUR MORE ON THE ADJOINING SILL. IF THE HYPOTENUSE WAS FIVE UNITS, THE SILL CORNER WAS SQUARE. IF NOT, A FEW WHACKS WITH A COMMANDER WOULD PERSUADE THE SILLS TO FORM A NINETY-DEGREE ANGLE. IF SO, THE DIAGONALS BETWEEN THE CORNERS SHOULD BE EQUAL.

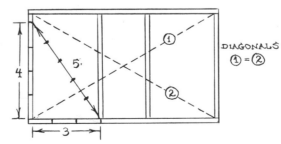

DIAGONALS ① = ②

LEVELS

Houses~and of course the people who lived in them~ should be honest and "on the level," as well as "on the square." The eighteenth-century level had its wooden arm at ninety degrees to the base. From it a lead weight was suspended on a string. A timber was truly level when the plumb string lined up with the center base mark. Without perfectly horizontal sills, all the timber joinings that followed would be out of kilter.

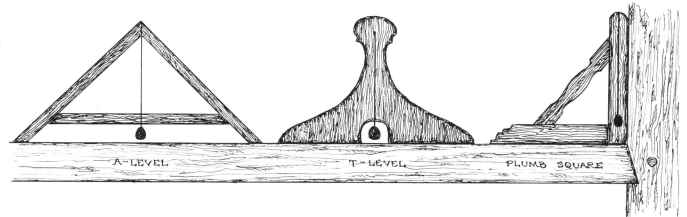

A-LEVEL   T-LEVEL   PLUMB SQUARE

CROWBARS

Heavy timber could be levered into position with these 4-foot-long iron persuaders. Out-of-level sills were raised enough to wedge chunks of stone into the dry-laid foundation beneath.

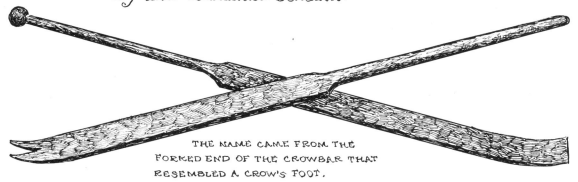

THE NAME CAME FROM THE FORKED END OF THE CROWBAR THAT RESEMBLED A CROW'S FOOT.

DOVETAILED JOISTS

To the master joiners, the dovetail joint looked much like the tail of a dove in flight. This remarkable joint could be simply lowered into the sill mortises without dissembling. Once wedged in place, any outward pull from the sills would only lock the dovetail more firmly in place. Unlike in the use of other joints, there was no need for pegging.

Floor joists must have given the post-and-beam builders a degree of pleasure. The log need only be debarked and a single face hewn to receive the flooring. Often the under ends of the joists were beveled to relieve a degree of stress at the dovetail junction.

STRESS

STRESS

SILL

29

The girders~ those weight~bearing big brothers to the joists~ required extra sill support with housed dovetail joints. It was an American original, and would later be invaluable when the summer beam was lowered and tied into the bent sections.

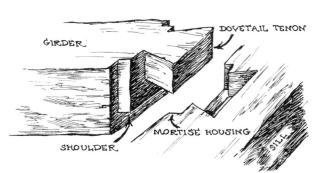

GIRDER

DOVETAIL TENON

SHOULDER

MORTISE HOUSING

SILL

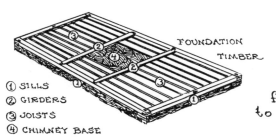

FOUNDATION TIMBER

① SILLS
② GIRDERS
③ JOISTS
④ CHIMNEY BASE

BENTS

Bents were preassembled sections that made up the width of the frame. Usually there were four~ the two ends and two like sections between them. The bent members were joined flat on the foundation timber and in position to be raised in place.

KNEE BRACE

PLATE

CROSS BEAM

POST

A TYPICAL BENT WITH ITS JOINED MEMBERS

POST TENON

SILL

CORNER MORTISE

SHOULDERED
MORTISE AND TENON

"RAISIN' DAY"

Everything was in readiness. It might well have taken a year since the first tree was felled to this day when a new American landmark was created. Being a good neighbor never meant more than on raising day. By dawn the villagers had largely gathered at the building site with their hearth-cooked victuals, drink, gossip, good will, music-makers~ and above all, plenty of muscle. There was the same anticipation of later Independence Day celebrations, for these were special times to never forget.

The bents were positioned on the temporary boards that covered the flooring timber. Hard by were stacked, numbered frame pieces that included the connecting girts that would secure the bents, the corner braces, the second floor and attic joists, the summer beams, and the rafters that would be raised, joined and seated to receive their share of purlins. All this took the organization of a field general who had the know-how of a master framer and a keen eye for any pitfalls that might lie ahead. Usually the responsibility fell upon the shoulders of the head carpenter.

IN THIS EXPANDED VIEW, THE BENTS ARE STACKED ON THE TEMPORARY DECKING, IN POSITION FOR THE RAISING. THE CORNER SILLS WERE BLOCKED TO PREVENT THE POSTS FROM SLIDING OFF THE DECK AS THE BENT WAS RAISED. A SAFETY ROPE WAS TIED TO THE PLATE TO PREVENT THE RAISED BENT FROM FALLING FORWARD.

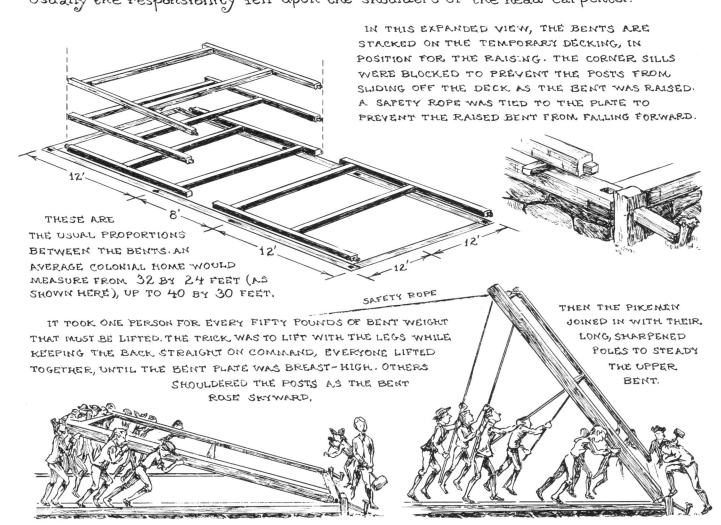

THESE ARE THE USUAL PROPORTIONS BETWEEN THE BENTS. AN AVERAGE COLONIAL HOME WOULD MEASURE FROM 32 BY 24 FEET (AS SHOWN HERE), UP TO 40 BY 30 FEET.

IT TOOK ONE PERSON FOR EVERY FIFTY POUNDS OF BENT WEIGHT THAT MUST BE LIFTED. THE TRICK WAS TO LIFT WITH THE LEGS WHILE KEEPING THE BACK STRAIGHT ON COMMAND, EVERYONE LIFTED TOGETHER, UNTIL THE BENT PLATE WAS BREAST-HIGH. OTHERS SHOULDERED THE POSTS AS THE BENT ROSE SKYWARD,

SAFETY ROPE

THEN THE PIKEMEN JOINED IN WITH THEIR LONG, SHARPENED POLES TO STEADY THE UPPER BENT.

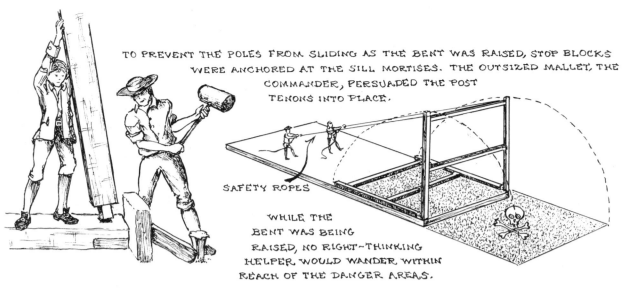

TO PREVENT THE POLES FROM SLIDING AS THE BENT WAS RAISED, STOP BLOCKS WERE ANCHORED AT THE SILL MORTISES. THE OUTSIZED MALLET, THE COMMANDER, PERSUADED THE POST TENONS INTO PLACE.

SAFETY ROPES

WHILE THE BENT WAS BEING RAISED, NO RIGHT~THINKING HELPER WOULD WANDER WITHIN REACH OF THE DANGER AREAS.

GIN POLES

Willing hands raised the one-story bent for such as a Cape Codder without benefit of mechanical devices. But erecting a weighty two-story bent of heavy timber was quite another problem.

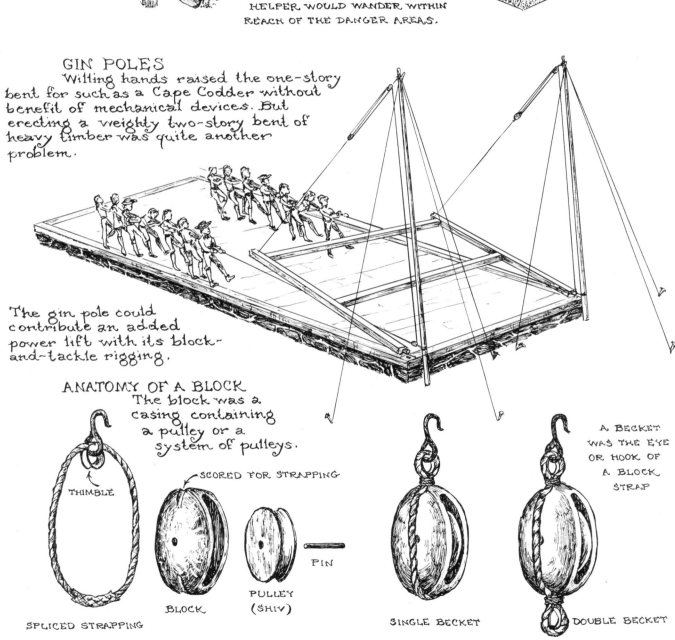

The gin pole could contribute an added power lift with its block-and-tackle rigging.

ANATOMY OF A BLOCK

The block was a casing containing a pulley or a system of pulleys.

THIMBLE

SPLICED STRAPPING

SCORED FOR STRAPPING

BLOCK

PULLEY (SHIV)

PIN

SINGLE BECKET

A BECKET WAS THE EYE OR HOOK OF A BLOCK STRAP

DOUBLE BECKET

TACKLE

A rope and its system of pulleys made up the tackle. The increased power advantage depended on the number of ropes supporting the movable block.

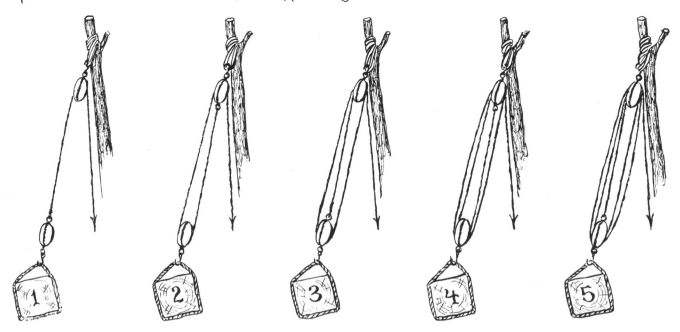

THE FIRST TACKLE HAS NO ADVANTAGE, FOR THE LIFT AND THE PULL ARE EQUAL. THE LAST TACKLE HAS FIVE ROPES TO THE MOVABLE BLOCK AND THEREFORE SUPPLIED FIVE TIMES THE LIFT POWER AS THE PULL. REGARDLESS OF THE NUMBER OF PULLEYS USED IN THE STATIONARY AND MOVABLE BLOCKS, THE GIN POLE HAD TO BE TALL ENOUGH TO LIFT THE TACKLE ABOVE THE RAISED BENT. TODAY, A CRANE IS A LATER ALTERNATIVE TO THE OLD MUSCLE AND GIN-POLE COMBINATION.

PLUMB BOB OR PLUMMET

Before the now upright bent could be secured with temporary braces, it had to be plumbed to be certain it stood perfectly vertical. To do so, a plumb bob was suspended from a cord. Originally of lead, its name came from the Latin "plumbum." The simple device not only checked the perpendicularity of the posts with the sills, but also the horizontality of such surfaces as the girts and plates when the plumb bob was hung from a framework (page 29).

CHECKING THE VERTICAL

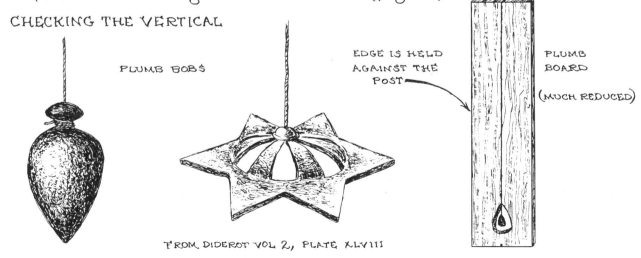

PLUMB BOBS

EDGE IS HELD AGAINST THE POST

PLUMB BOARD

(MUCH REDUCED)

FROM DIDEROT VOL 2, PLATE XLVIII

JOINING THE BENTS

The front and back girts were raised and their tenons were eased into the corner post mortises at the same time as the knee braces were positioned. Then the pins were pounded home.
The next step was to tilt the second bent off enough to be joined with the girt and braces. Once pegged, the box-like partial frame was ready to be locked together forever with a summer beam.

SECOND BENT

SUMMER BEAM

This massive weight-bearing timber~ often the heaviest of the entire framework~ tied the two bents together. The name had nothing to do with the seasons. Likely it was a corruption of the old English word "sumpter," meaning a pack horse or mule that carried heavy loads. So it was with the summer beam, for it carried the second floor joists as a midway support.

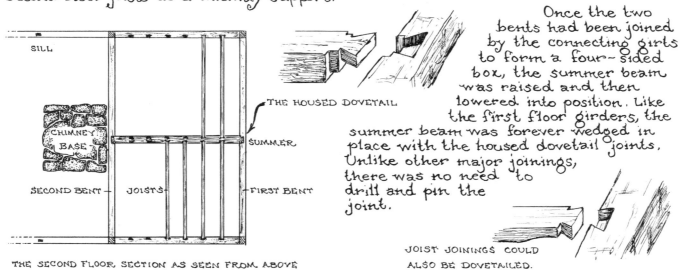

SILL

CHIMNEY BASE

THE HOUSED DOVETAIL

SUMMER

SECOND BENT — JOISTS — FIRST BENT

THE SECOND FLOOR SECTION AS SEEN FROM ABOVE

Once the two bents had been joined by the connecting girts to form a four-sided box, the summer beam was raised and then lowered into position. Like the first floor girders, the summer beam was forever wedged in place with the housed dovetail joints. Unlike other major joinings, there was no need to drill and pin the joint.

JOIST JOININGS COULD ALSO BE DOVETAILED.

Because the summer beam was of such size, it projected well into the room below. A few runs with a molding plane could turn it into an architectural feature. The simplest edge dressing was a beveled chamfer. The ogee and the head were a bit more elegant. Whatever the design, the decorative molding ended with various chamfer stops.

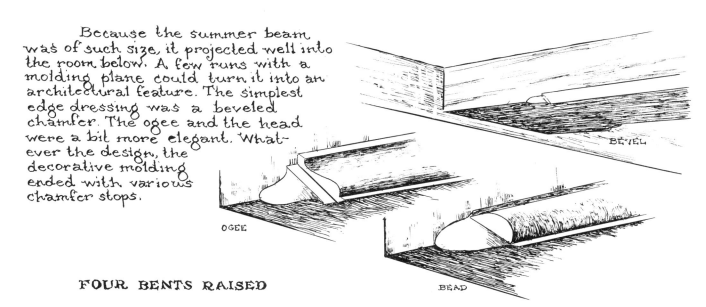

BEVEL

OGEE

BEAD

FOUR BENTS RAISED

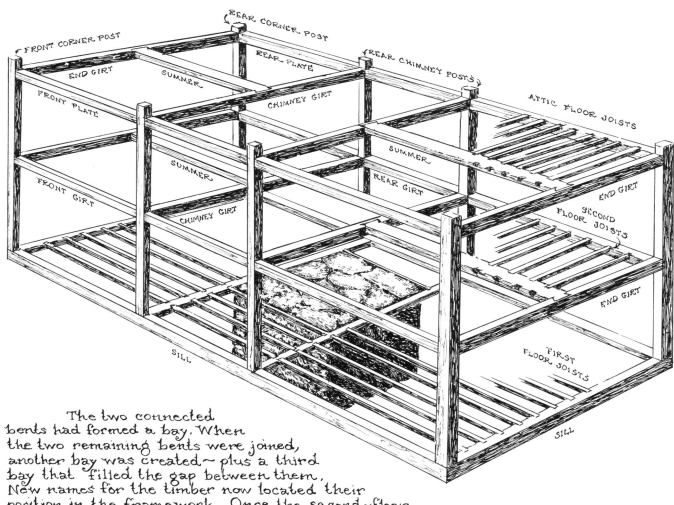

FRONT CORNER POST

REAR CORNER POST

REAR PLATE

REAR CHIMNEY POSTS

END GIRT

SUMMER

ATTIC FLOOR JOISTS

FRONT PLATE

CHIMNEY GIRT

FRONT GIRT

SUMMER

SUMMER

REAR GIRT

END GIRT

SECOND FLOOR JOISTS

CHIMNEY GIRT

END GIRT

SILL

FIRST FLOOR JOISTS

SILL

The two connected bents had formed a bay. When the two remaining bents were joined, another bay was created ~ plus a third bay that filled the gap between them. New names for the timber now located their position in the framework. Once the second-floor ceiling summer beams and the plates had been lowered into place, all that was needed to complete the frame was the capping with the roofing timbers.

35

"RAISING THE ROOF"

As with the second floor, the joists were tapped into the mortises of the summer beam and the flanking front and rear plates. The last of the framing timbers were stacked and ready to be hoisted to the temporary attic decking. These were the rafters, collar ties, and purlins that had earlier been fitted together and then disassembled.

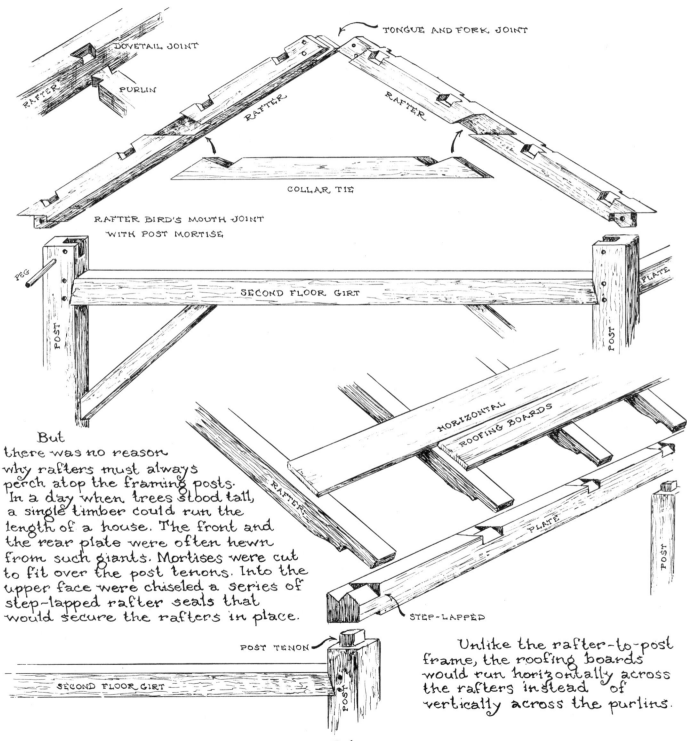

DOVETAIL JOINT

RAFTER

PURLIN

TONGUE AND FORK JOINT

RAFTER

RAFTER

COLLAR TIE

RAFTER BIRD'S MOUTH JOINT WITH POST MORTISE

PEG

POST

SECOND FLOOR GIRT

POST

PLATE

HORIZONTAL ROOFING BOARDS

RAFTERS

PLATE

POST

STEP-LAPPED

POST TENON

SECOND FLOOR GIRT

POST

But there was no reason why rafters must always perch atop the framing posts. In a day when trees stood tall, a single timber could run the length of a house. The front and the rear plate were often hewn from such giants. Mortises were cut to fit over the post tenons. Into the upper face were chiseled a series of step-lapped rafter seals that would secure the rafters in place.

Unlike the rafter-to-post frame, the roofing boards would run horizontally across the rafters instead of vertically across the purlins.

36

NOTE ON RAFTER RAISING

RAFTER TO POST

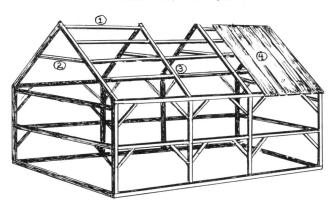

RAFTER TO PLATE

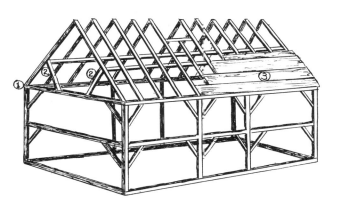

① PURLINS AT THE RAFTER PEAKS SERVE AS RIDGEPOLES BEFORE 1800.

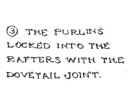

② COLLAR BEAMS PREVENTED THE SPREADING AND SAGGING OF RAFTERS FROM WIND AND THE WEIGHT OF SNOW. TWO JOINTS WERE FAVORED:

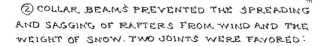

LAPPED HALF DOVETAIL   PINNED TENON

③ THE PURLINS LOCKED INTO THE RAFTERS WITH THE DOVETAIL JOINT.

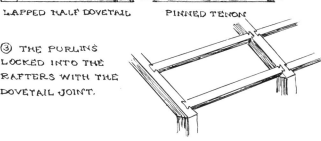

④ THE ROOFING BOARDS WERE NAILED VERTICALLY TO THE PURLINS.

① CORNER JOINTS TYING THE POST TO GIRT AND PLATE WERE:

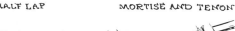

CORNER HALF LAP   MORTISE AND TENON

② SUPPORT PURLINS REPLACED THE COLLAR TIES FOR RAFTER SUPPORT.

③ THE ROOFING BOARDS WERE NAILED HORIZONTALLY TO THE RAFTERS.

WHATEVER THE RAFTER ARRANGEMENT, EACH PAIR OF RAFTERS WAS JOINED AND PEGGED ON THE ATTIC BOARDS: ONE END PAIR OF RAFTERS WAS RAISED AGAINST POST STOPS, PLUMBED, PEGGED, AND TEMPORARILY BRACED. WHEN THE SECOND PAIR WAS RAISED AND BRACED, THE PURLINS COULD BE LOCKED INTO PLACE. THE REMAINING RAFTER PAIRS WERE RAISED AND JOINED IN LIKE MANNER. ALL THAT WAS NEEDED WAS A SMALL PINE NAILED TO A RAFTER ~ A TRIBUTE TO THE TREES AND THE NEIGHBORS WHO MADE THIS STOUT FRAMEWORK POSSIBLE.

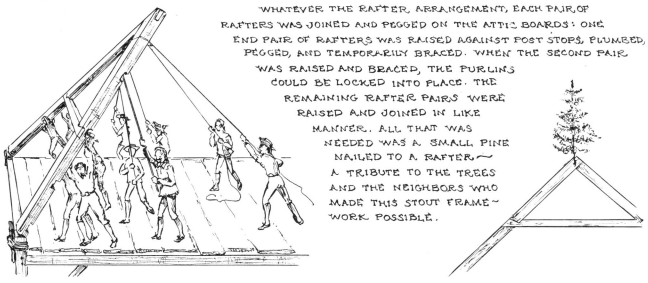

BOARDING THE FRAME

"Raisin' Day" had ended with an assortment of tired muscles, Yankee wit and tall stories, husky appetites for hearth cooking at its best and dancing into the night. But by dawn the housewrights were back on the job, ready to sheath their new frame creation. While boards had already been put to use as temporary decking, there would be many wagon loads needed from the sawyers. By the early 1700s, there was a trend toward sheathing the roof and siding with sawn boards before nailing home the shingles and clapboards.

THE PIT SAW

Sawing logs lengthwise into boards called for a husky broad-bladed saw with teeth like small chisels. This tool's design (ripping blades held taut in a wooden framework) hadn't changed since the fifteenth century. Shortly after the colonists arrived at Jamestown and Plymouth, the casting technique of steel had been improved. As a result, a new pit saw came into being ~ one that needed no framework to keep tension on a blade that was now considerably stronger. Colonists called it a whip or open pit saw; by the mid~eighteenth century, it had become the favorite.

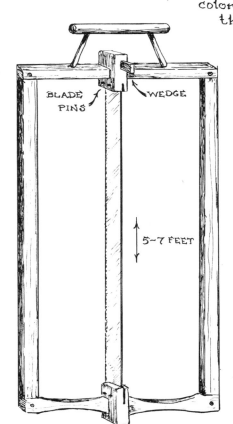

BLADE PINS — WEDGE

5-7 FEET

THE FRAMED PIT SAW
(FORTRESS LOUISBOURG, NOVA SCOTIA)

TILLER HANDLE

WHIP OR OPEN PIT SAW WITH TAPERED BLADE

CHISEL TOOTH

PIT SAW TEETH POINTED DOWNWARD TO RIP ABOUT AN INCH INTO THE LENGTH OF THE LOG WITH EACH STROKE. A HOLLOW GULLET IN FRONT OF EVERY TOOTH GAVE MORE ROOM FOR THE PILE-UP OF SAWDUST SHAVINGS.

THE BLADE HAD TO BE DISENGAGED WHEN THE CUT NEARED THE PIT SUPPORT OR THE TRESTLE. TO FREE THE FRAMED BLADE, THE TENSION WEDGE AND THE TWO PINS WERE REMOVED. THE WHIP BLADE CHANGE WAS MUCH EASIER, FOR THE BOX HANDLE AT THE TAPERED LOWER END ONLY NEEDED TO HAVE ITS WEDGE REMOVED BEFORE REPOSITIONING THE BLADE.

BOX HANDLE

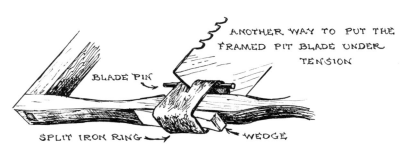

ANOTHER WAY TO PUT THE FRAMED PIT BLADE UNDER TENSION

BLADE PIN

SPLIT IRON RING — WEDGE

THE WEDGED BOX HANDLE

PIT SILL

TOMMY BAR TURNED ROLLER

SAWYER'S VIEW FROM THE TOP

EACH OF THE SNAPPED GUIDELINES WAS SAWED TO THE PIT ROLLER OR THE CRUTCH.

WHIP SAW

FRAME SAW

BOX HANDLE

THE ROLLER NEAREST THE CUTS WAS MOVED OUTWARD TO A FOOT OR SO FROM THE LOG'S END.

TO CONTINUE EACH CUT DOWN THE LENGTH OF THE LOG, THE BLADE MUST BE FREED TO INSERT IT ON THE INNER SIDE OF THE PIT ROLLER OR CRUTCH. THAT WAS EASY ENOUGH WITH THE WHIPSAW BLADE, FOR ONLY THE BOX-HANDLE WEDGE NEEDED TO BE KNOCKED OUT BEFORE PUSHING THE TAPERED END OF THE BLADE INTO THE CUT.

THE SAWYER'S HANDLE, THE TILLER, COULD STEER A WAYWARD BUT FLEXIBLE WHIP-SAW BLADE BACK ON COURSE IF GIVEN A SLIGHT TWIST BACK TOWARD THE CHALK LINE.

ON THE OTHER HAND, REMOVING THE BLADE FROM THE FRAME SAW CALLED FOR A TIME-CONSUMING REMOVAL OF ALL THE WEDGES AND PINS BEFORE THE BLADE COULD BE REINSERTED.

PIT SILL

THE CUT OR KERF WAS CONTINUED TO THE FAR ROLLER, LEAVING ABOUT 6 INCHES OF UNCUT LOG. SAWING THE FULL LENGTH OF EACH BOARD WOULD SOON LEAVE THE SAWYER STANDING ON AIR. WEDGES DRIVEN INTO EACH CUT PREVENTED ANY BINDING ON THE BLADE. THEN THE SAW WAS DISENGAGED, THE BLADE REINSERTED INTO THE NEIGHBORING CUT, AND THE SAWING RESUMED.

FINALLY, THE FAR ROLLER WAS TURNED FORWARD, WELL UNDER THE CUTS. THE DOG WAS REMOVED AND THE CROSSCUT BOW SAW USED TO FREE THE BOARDS. THEY WERE READY FOR STACKING AND AIR-DRYING.

PIT SILL

Pit sawing was a two-man operation. The log to be sawed was supported over a pit. Larger operations such as ship-building lumberyards would use elevated trestles, such as was shown in this eighteenth-century plate. The sawyer stood on the log and guided the blade along snapped chalk lines. Below, the pitman, aided by the weight of the saw and gravity, pulled the saw downward. This unenviable chore brought down a shower of sawdust with each stroke. His broadbrimmed hat was a must. Perhaps the saying "it's the pits" originated from the pitman's lowly position.

PLATE I, MENOISERIE, VOLUME VII, DIDEROT
DICTIONNAIRE DES SCIENCES, PARIS, 1790

THE PITSAW IN ACTION

WITH THE LOG POSITIONED ON ROLLERS, THE BARK WAS SKINNED OFF WITH THE SPUD.

CHALK OR CHARCOAL LINES WERE SNAPPED AS GUIDES FOR A SAWYER.

THE LOG WAS ROLLED OVER AND ONTO TWO JOIST ROLLERS AND SECURED WITH A DOG.

THE PIT

THE LOG PROJECTED 3 OR 4 FEET OVER THE SUPPORT, READY FOR SAWING.

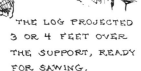

TRESTLE

CRUTCH

AN ALTERNATIVE WAS A TRESTLE ~ MUCH LIKE AN OUTSIZED SAWHORSE ~ AT ONE END AND A MOVABLE CRUTCH 3 OR 4 FEET FROM ITS END. IT TOOK REAL MANPOWER TO POSITION THE LOG.

THE SAWYER STOOD ON THE LOG, PUSHING DOWN AND GUIDING THE CUT ON THE DOWNSTROKE. THE PITMAN KEPT THE BLADE PLUMB WHILE DOWNWARD TO ADVANCE THE BLADE~ ON THE RETURN STROKE. THE SAWYER RAISED THE HANDLE TO SHOULDER HEIGHT AS THE PITMAN PUSHED UP AND SLIGHTLY BACKWARD TO PREVENT ANY FRICTION DRAG.

THE SAWMILL AT WORK

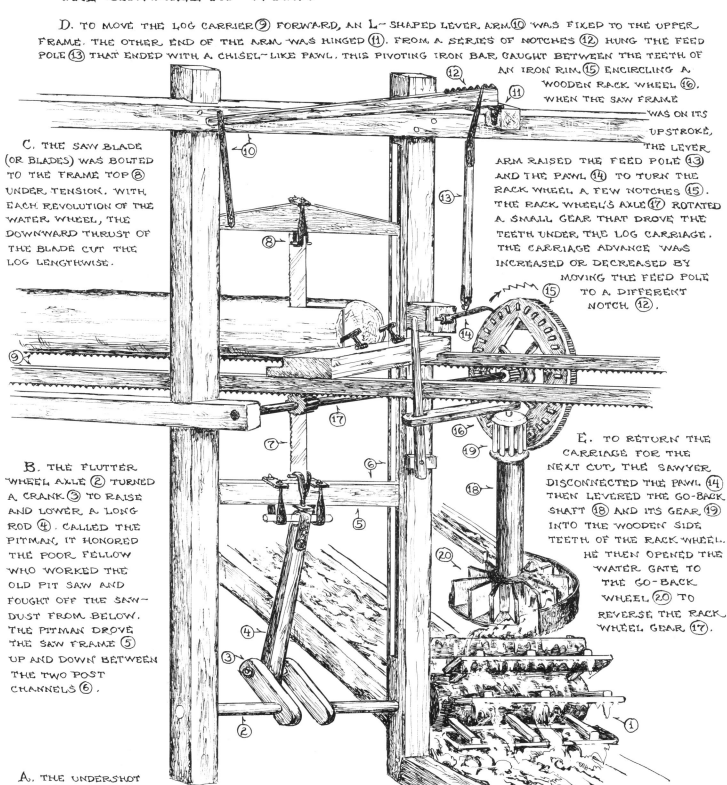

D. TO MOVE THE LOG CARRIER ⑨ FORWARD, AN L-SHAPED LEVER ARM ⑩ WAS FIXED TO THE UPPER FRAME. THE OTHER END OF THE ARM WAS HINGED ⑪. FROM A SERIES OF NOTCHES ⑫ HUNG THE FEED POLE ⑬ THAT ENDED WITH A CHISEL-LIKE PAWL. THIS PIVOTING IRON BAR CAUGHT BETWEEN THE TEETH OF AN IRON RIM ⑮ ENCIRCLING A WOODEN RACK WHEEL ⑯. WHEN THE SAW FRAME WAS ON ITS UPSTROKE, THE LEVER ARM RAISED THE FEED POLE ⑬ AND THE PAWL ⑭ TO TURN THE RACK WHEEL A FEW NOTCHES ⑮. THE RACK WHEEL'S AXLE ⑰ ROTATED A SMALL GEAR THAT DROVE THE TEETH UNDER THE LOG CARRIAGE. THE CARRIAGE ADVANCE WAS INCREASED OR DECREASED BY MOVING THE FEED POLE TO A DIFFERENT NOTCH ⑫.

C. THE SAW BLADE (OR BLADES) WAS BOLTED TO THE FRAME TOP ⑧ UNDER TENSION. WITH EACH REVOLUTION OF THE WATER WHEEL, THE DOWNWARD THRUST OF THE BLADE CUT THE LOG LENGTHWISE.

B. THE FLUTTER WHEEL AXLE ② TURNED A CRANK ③ TO RAISE AND LOWER A LONG ROD ④. CALLED THE PITMAN, IT HONORED THE POOR FELLOW WHO WORKED THE OLD PIT SAW AND FOUGHT OFF THE SAW-DUST FROM BELOW. THE PITMAN DROVE THE SAW FRAME ⑤ UP AND DOWN BETWEEN THE TWO POST CHANNELS ⑥.

E. TO RETURN THE CARRIAGE FOR THE NEXT CUT, THE SAWYER DISCONNECTED THE PAWL ⑭ THEN LEVERED THE GO-BACK SHAFT ⑱ AND ITS GEAR ⑲ INTO THE WOODEN SIDE TEETH OF THE RACK WHEEL. HE THEN OPENED THE WATER GATE TO THE GO-BACK WHEEL ⑳ TO REVERSE THE RACK WHEEL GEAR ⑰.

A. THE UNDERSHOT WHEEL ①, THE USUAL DRIVING FORCE FOR A SAWMILL, SOUNDED LIKE FLUTTERING WINGS WHEN THE STREAM OF WATER REVOLVED THE PADDLES.

41

SHINGLES

SEVENTEENTH CENTURY HALF~TIMBERED
ENGLISH HOUSE WITH THATCHED ROOF

The early colonists carried on the old English tradition of roof thatching. The topping of bound bundles of reeds and straw required a sharply pitched roof~up to sixty degrees~to hurry off soaking rains. Rows of horizontal sticks were nailed to the rafters to secure the thatching. But well before the last quarter of the seventeenth century had begun, blustery winds and downpours on this side of the Atlantic could turn the straw bundles into overhead sponges.

Shingles split from oak, cypress, chestnut, and white pine were the weather-worthy answers. When laid in overlapping rows and nailed to the 1-by-3-inch thatch purlins, water quickly drained down the fibrous grooves of the split surfaces. Underneath, a free circulation of air prevented rot. A more gentle rafter slope of forty-five degrees was all that was needed. The new roofing could well last a lifetime. Before many years, the entire framework would be sheathed in sawn boards, making the thatch purlins obsolete.

FROE AND MAUL

These riving tools were introduced on pages 24 and 25 with the making of timber pegs (treenails or "trunnels"). Following the rule of thumb, the wood was worked when green and shingled when seasoned. The splitting technique did vary, according to the kind of wood being used.

STRAIGHT~GRAINED, KNOT~FREE
SECTIONS WERE CUT FROM THE LOG.
24~TO~30~INCH LENGTHS WERE USUAL.

HEARTWOOD

SAPWOOD

OAK

OAK HAD UNDESIRABLE PORTIONS THAT MUST BE REMOVED. THE HEARTWOOD WAS BRITTLE AND HARD. A WROUGHT IRON NAIL WOULD BUCKLE AFTER SEVERAL BLOWS. THE OUTER RINGS OF SAPWOOD ROTTED QUICKLY AND HAD NO PLACE IN WEATHER BOARDING.

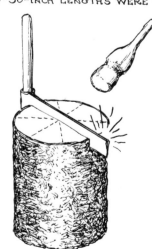

THE PIECE WAS UPENDED
AND SPLIT INTO EQUAL
SECTIONS CALLED BILLETS.

A LARGE~DIAMETER CHUNK
MIGHT NEED WEDGES TO
SPLIT OUT THE BILLETS.

4 INCHES ±

THE SAPWOOD AND BARK WERE
RIVED OFF THE BILLET.

EACH BILLET WAS SPLIT DEAD~CENTER TO GIVE TWO EQUAL HALVES; EACH HALF WAS THEN RIVED AGAIN TO GIVE FOUR WEDGE~SHAPED PIECES. IF THE SPLIT WAS NEARER AN EDGE THAN THE CENTER, IT WAS APT TO CROSS FIBERS AND DRIFT TOWARD THE THINNER PIECE.

DRIFT

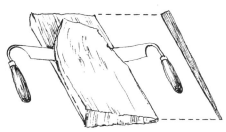

THE WEDGE~SHAPED SHINGLE MUST BE FEATHERED WITH A DRAW KNIFE. THE SMOOTHED SURFACE WOULD FORM THE UNDER~PART OF THE SHINGLE AND THE SPLIT SURFACE WOULD FACE UP TO DRAIN THE RAINS.

OAK BILLETS CERTAINLY SPLIT WELL WITH THE FROE AND REPELLED INSECTS AND ROT HANDILY, BUT THE RIVED WEDGE SHAPE MADE OAK A BETTER CLAPBOARD THAN A SHINGLE.

The first trial slices of cedar, cypress, chestnut, and white pine must have been a happy surprise. These woods had none of oak's sapwood or heartwood, and no trimming was necessary. They need not be rived into wedge-shaped billets, for the shingles could be split parallel to each other. Further, the fact that an off-center split sheared off toward the thinner side could now be used to advantage with cedar, cypress, chestnut, and white pine. When the froe was driven in an inch or so from a riven face and then levered, the split crossed fibers and on down to produce a neatly tapered shingle. Any high spots could be trimmed off with a draw knife.

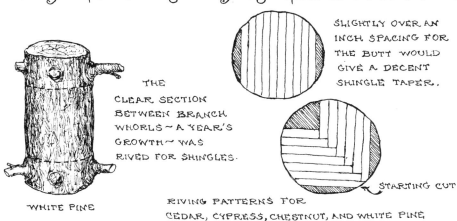

THE CLEAR SECTION BETWEEN BRANCH WHORLS ~ A YEAR'S GROWTH ~ WAS RIVED FOR SHINGLES.

WHITE PINE

SLIGHTLY OVER AN INCH SPACING FOR THE BUTT WOULD GIVE A DECENT SHINGLE TAPER.

STARTING CUT

RIVING PATTERNS FOR CEDAR, CYPRESS, CHESTNUT, AND WHITE PINE

THE SPLIT FIBER GROOVES MADE FINE DRAINAGE CHANNELS.

24~30 INCHES

AFTER EACH SHINGLE WAS LEVERED FREE, THE LOG SECTION WAS TURNED UPSIDE~DOWN TO KEEP THE TAPER.

RIVING SHINGLES WAS A GOOD WINTER SIT~DOWN CHORE FOR YOUNGSTERS AND OLDSTERS. PRACTICED HANDS COULD TURN OUT UPWARD TO FIVE HUNDRED SHINGLES A DAY. RIVEN GREEN, THEY WOULD BE STACKED AND DRY ENOUGH FOR WARM WEATHER ROOFING.

43

THE SHINGLING HATCHET

HAMMER POLL

BROAD BLADE BEVELED ON ONE SIDE ONLY

The early thatched roofs needed no special tool such as this. When wooden shingles became popular, the flat-sided hatchet was developed for hewing straight and square edges. It worked much like a small broadax. Shingles could be trimmed or divided on the roof. Upended, the hammer could drive the shingle nail. The wrist thong kept the hatchet from tumbling to the ground below.

The now-familiar claw atop the poll or the notched blade were unknown to the eighteenth-century builder. Not until about 1830, when cut nails had become plentiful, were the nail pullers added to the shingling hatchet.

5"

THIS DAINTY SHINGLING HATCHET IS PROBABLY POST-REVOLUTIONARY. IT HAS A BEVEL ON BOTH SIDES TO GIVE A KNIFE EDGE. THE POLL BALANCES THE BLADE NICELY.

A FEW CHOPS WITH THE SHINGLING HATCHET TRIMMED AND SQUARED THE BARK EDGES. SINCE SHINGLES WIDER THAN 7 TO 8 INCHES WOULD SWELL CONSIDERABLY WHEN WET, THEY EXPANDED TOWARD THEIR NEIGHBORS AND BUCKLED. THEREFORE SHINGLES OF LARGER SIZES SHOULD BE SPLIT IN HALF.

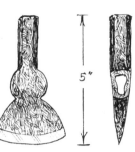

THE FEATHER END OF THE SHINGLES MIGHT WELL SPLIT WHEN DRIVEN HOME. SEASONED SHINGLES WERE LESS APT TO SPLIT THAN THOSE OF GREEN (NEWLY CUT) WOOD. IT WAS THEREFORE PRUDENT TO USE A GIMLET OR A WEDGE-SHAPED NAIL.

SHINGLING NAILS

THE GIMLET

This mini-sized auger had a half-cylindrical body with sharpened edges. It ended with a rounded or pointed nose to start the hole without wandering. The nose first forced the wood fibers apart and then trimmed out the hole with the cutting edges. A nail could then be driven in without splitting the shingle apart.

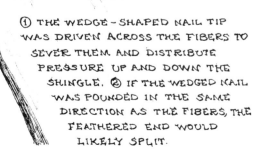

① THE WEDGE-SHAPED NAIL TIP WAS DRIVEN ACROSS THE FIBERS TO SEVER THEM AND DISTRIBUTE PRESSURE UP AND DOWN THE SHINGLE. ② IF THE WEDGED NAIL WAS POUNDED IN THE SAME DIRECTION AS THE FIBERS, THE FEATHERED END WOULD LIKELY SPLIT.

44

You may recall the three purlin-to-rafter framing for colonial roofs.

WHEN THATCHING WAS FOUND TO BE IMPRACTICAL, THE 1-BY-3-INCH PURLINS, SPACED EVERY 8 INCHES ON THE RAFTERS, WERE USED FOR NAILING THE WOODEN SHINGLES.

RAFTERS WITH SUPPORT PURLINS WERE BOARDED HORIZONTALLY.

RAFTERS WITH DOVETAILED PURLINS WERE BOARDED VERTICALLY.

By the early 1700s, pit saws and sawmills were turning out boards in great plenty. Rejects with splits and knots could be used as outside sheathing. Nailed to the frame before being covered with shingles or clapboards, they gave added insulation and weatherproofing. The old thatching purlins faded into history.

ALL ABOUT EAVES

It had always been prudent to extend the roof edge a foot or so to protect the siding below. Still, those unfaced eaves just wouldn't do once the colonies became more affluent. By extending the girt over the front plate, a second plate could be added to support the rafter feet. Once boxed in and embellished with moldings, the homestead took on a more elegant, classical look. But such niceties would have to wait until the roof was shingled and the siding protected with weatherboards.

THE DUTCH INFLUENCE IN NEW YORK AND NEW JERSEY FEATURED GRACEFUL EAVES THAT CURVED 2 OR MORE FEET BEYOND THE FRONT AND BACK OF THE HOUSE.

SECOND PLATE

GIRT

FIRST PLATE

LAYING THE SHINGLES

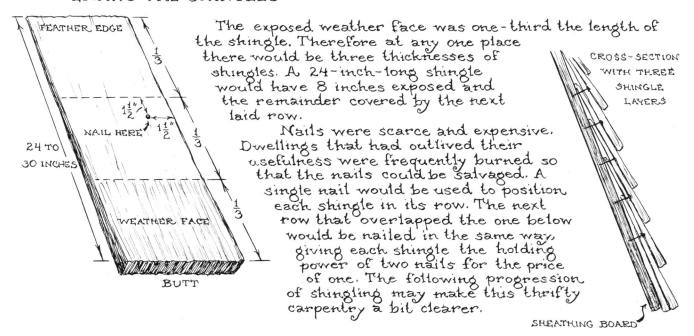

FEATHER EDGE

1/3

1 1/2"

NAIL HERE 1 1/2"

1/3

24 TO 30 INCHES

WEATHER FACE

1/3

BUTT

CROSS-SECTION WITH THREE SHINGLE LAYERS

SHEATHING BOARD

The exposed weather face was one-third the length of the shingle. Therefore at any one place there would be three thicknesses of shingles. A 24-inch-long shingle would have 8 inches exposed and the remainder covered by the next laid row.

Nails were scarce and expensive. Dwellings that had outlived their usefulness were frequently burned so that the nails could be salvaged. A single nail would be used to position each shingle in its row. The next row that overlapped the one below would be nailed in the same way, giving each shingle the holding power of two nails for the price of one. The following progression of shingling may make this thrifty carpentry a bit clearer.

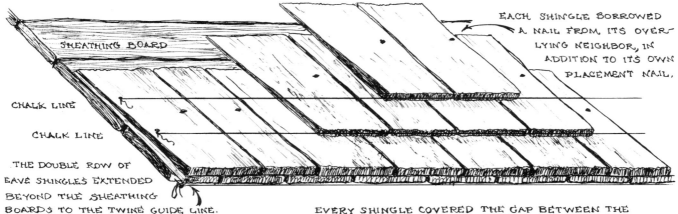

SHEATHING BOARD

EACH SHINGLE BORROWED A NAIL FROM ITS OVER-LYING NEIGHBOR, IN ADDITION TO ITS OWN PLACEMENT NAIL.

CHALK LINE

CHALK LINE

THE DOUBLE ROW OF EAVE SHINGLES EXTENDED BEYOND THE SHEATHING BOARDS TO THE TWINE GUIDE LINE.

EVERY SHINGLE COVERED THE GAP BETWEEN THE TWO SHINGLES BENEATH IT. FOR SEASONED SHINGLES, THE SPACE WAS $\frac{1}{4}$ INCH TO ALLOW FOR ANY SWELLING WHEN WET. GENERALLY ANY NAIL SHOULD BE $1\frac{1}{2}$ INCHES IN FROM THE SHINGLE BORDER TO BE PROTECTED BY THE OVERLYING SHINGLE.

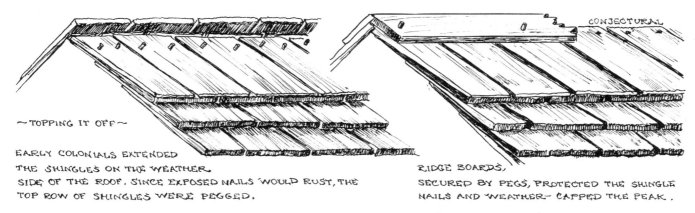

~TOPPING IT OFF~

EARLY COLONIALS EXTENDED THE SHINGLES ON THE WEATHER SIDE OF THE ROOF. SINCE EXPOSED NAILS WOULD RUST, THE TOP ROW OF SHINGLES WERE PEGGED.

CONJECTURAL

RIDGE BOARDS, SECURED BY PEGS, PROTECTED THE SHINGLE NAILS AND WEATHER-CAPPED THE PEAK.

WEATHERBOARDS

The half timbered English house had real transplanting problems on this side of the Atlantic. The driving storms had underscored the need for sturdy wooden shingles rather than the traditional thatch. The clay and chopped straw filling between the supporting timber fared no better. The elements soon cracked and otherwise tormented the filler until it was clear that an outer protective covering was a must. Clapboards were the answer.

CLAPBOARDS. The word came from the German word "Klappholt" (klapper meant "clap" and holt meant "wood") and referred to the rived-oak lengths that would be worked into barrel staves. The colonists took the idea and ran with it.

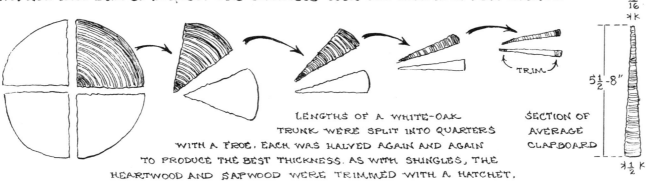

LENGTHS OF A WHITE-OAK TRUNK WERE SPLIT INTO QUARTERS WITH A FROE. EACH WAS HALVED AGAIN AND AGAIN TO PRODUCE THE BEST THICKNESS. AS WITH SHINGLES, THE HEARTWOOD AND SAPWOOD WERE TRIMMED WITH A HATCHET.

TRIM

$\frac{3}{16}$"

$5\frac{1}{2}$-8"

$\frac{1}{2}$

SECTION OF AVERAGE CLAPBOARD

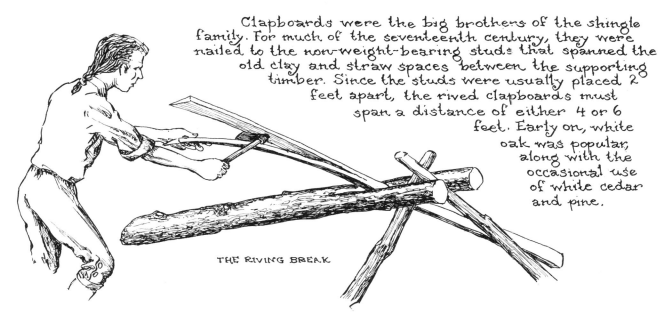

Clapboards were the big brothers of the shingle family. For much of the seventeenth century, they were nailed to the non-weight-bearing studs that spanned the old clay and straw spaces between the supporting timber. Since the studs were usually placed 2 feet apart, the rived clapboards must span a distance of either 4 or 6 feet. Early on, white oak was popular, along with the occasional use of white cedar and pine.

THE RIVING BREAK

THE RIVING BREAK

Although the same froe and maul were used in a like way for both clapboard and shingles, the longer length of the clapboard called for a more practiced hand~ and a riving break. It was nothing more than the forked limb of a felled tree, raised to the horizontal by sturdy crossed sticks within the fork. The riving break could be raised by bringing the crossed sticks closer together and nearer to the base of the fork. To lower, the sticks were spread and moved away from the base.

LOWERING THE BREAK   RAISING THE BREAK

If a split began to run off to one side, it would continue to do so as the froe was twisted. The thinner side would bend more, stretch its fibers, and become the path of least resistance. To correct the way-ward split, the thicker half was placed downward in the riving break, then bent downward with one hand. The froe could then be advanced as it was turned to and fro. The split would drift into the thicker half. The hand pressure was released as the wood separated down its center. Before riving either half into thinner halves, the future clapboard was inverted to split from the opposite end to even out any previous drifting.

NAILING THE RIVED CLAPBOARD

These early clapboards averaged 5 inches wide with 4 inches of "weather" or exposed surface. The ends were beveled and a single nail secured two ends to a stud.

STUDS

POST

CORNER BOARD

SAWN CLAPBOARDS

By the early 1700s, sawmills were turning out quantities of clapboards that ran as long as the length of the log. Throughout that century the builder had four types to consider. The trend toward an undersheathing of boards is shown in two of the sketches. White pine had become the favored wood for clapboards. As with shingles, pine was soft and easily worked, had no troublesome heartwood or sapwood, and actually was more enduring than oak when exposed to weather. White cedar, basswood, and hard pine also had their good points, but they were used to a lesser extent.

FROM THE LATE 1600s   FROM THE LATE 1600s   FROM THE EARLY 1700s   FROM THE MID 1700s

BEVELED EDGE ~ SOMETIMES USED ON SIDES AND BACK, OVERLAPPING CLAPBOARDS IN FRONT.

FEATHEREDGED CLAPBOARDS WERE NAILED TO A BOARD. UNDERSHEATHING WAS THE MOST FAVORED.

ORDINARY BOARDS OVERLAPPED THE ONE BELOW. A SIDE BEAD WAS OFTEN PLANED ABOVE THE EDGES.

A RABBET HELD THE OVERLAP, A SIDE BEAD DECORATES THE EDGES. LESS COMMON THAN FEATHEREDGED.

There was a trick to sawing a clapboard that was wedge-shaped rather than oblong on cross-section.

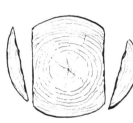
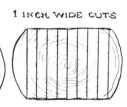

1 INCH WIDE CUTS

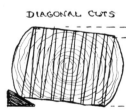

DIAGONAL CUTS

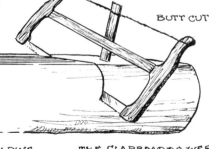

BUTT CUT

SIDE SLABS WERE CUT OFF AT THE SAWMILL OR SAWPIT.

THE LOG WAS TURNED AND A SERIES OF SAW CUTS WERE MADE JUST SHORT OF THE OPPOSITE END.

WITH THE UNCUT BUTT HOLDING THE SLOTTED LOG TOGETHER, THE LOG WAS TILTED WITH A WEDGE. VERTICAL CUTS ON THE DIAGONAL THEN GAVE FEATHEREDGED BOARDS.

THE CLAPBOARDS WERE RELEASED BY SAWING OFF THE UNWANTED END.

The rough-cut outer face must be dressed with a plane.

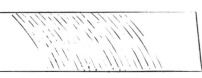

THE PIT SAW GAVE VARIED ANGLES AND WIDTHS.

THE SAWMILL PRODUCED REGULAR VERTICAL CUTS OF UNIFORM WIDTHS.

THE CIRCULAR SAW DID NOT PRODUCE ITS REGULAR ARCS OF UNIFORM WIDTHS UNTIL 1840.

THE JACK PLANE

Old-timers called this much-used tool a fore plane ~ and with good reason. The convex cutting edge of the iron could plough off such unwanted problems as clapboard saw marks before any finish planing. Being a convex shaver, the gently scooped path it left behind was pleasing to the eye and the touch. Running one's hand over the handplaned bottom of an eighteenth-century colonial drawer or table should prove the point. Usually the jack-planed clapboards were smooth enough to need no further finish work.

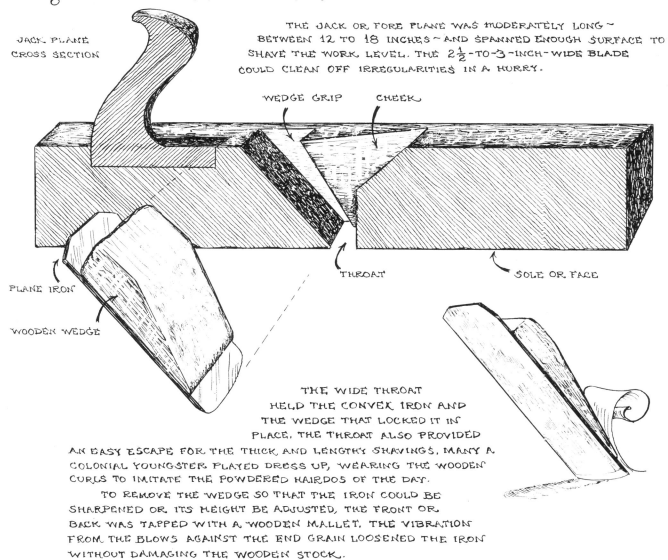

JACK PLANE
CROSS SECTION

THE JACK OR FORE PLANE WAS MODERATELY LONG ~ BETWEEN 12 TO 18 INCHES ~ AND SPANNED ENOUGH SURFACE TO SHAVE THE WORK LEVEL. THE 2½-TO-3-INCH-WIDE BLADE COULD CLEAN OFF IRREGULARITIES IN A HURRY.

WEDGE GRIP   CHEEK

PLANE IRON

WOODEN WEDGE

THROAT

SOLE OR FACE

THE WIDE THROAT HELD THE CONVEX IRON AND THE WEDGE THAT LOCKED IT IN PLACE. THE THROAT ALSO PROVIDED AN EASY ESCAPE FOR THE THICK AND LENGTHY SHAVINGS. MANY A COLONIAL YOUNGSTER PLAYED DRESS UP, WEARING THE WOODEN CURLS TO IMITATE THE POWDERED HAIRDOS OF THE DAY.

TO REMOVE THE WEDGE SO THAT THE IRON COULD BE SHARPENED OR ITS HEIGHT BE ADJUSTED, THE FRONT OR BACK WAS TAPPED WITH A WOODEN MALLET. THE VIBRATION FROM THE BLOWS AGAINST THE END GRAIN LOOSENED THE IRON WITHOUT DAMAGING THE WOODEN STOCK.

SIDING SIDELIGHTS

There was a notable exception to the clapboarding of the post-and-beam dwelling. The Long Island Dutch had expressed their individualism with gracefully extended eaves. They then extended the roofing shingles down to cover the siding. Such coverings gave a pleasing effect that was not lost on their neighbors. Soon many colonists in New Jersey and New York, along the Connecticut shoreline, and on to Cape Cod and the shore islands followed the example. Today it would be hard to imagine a homey Cape Cod homestead not being sided with its weathered-gray shingles.

SURFACING THE STUDS

Since the air between the posts and beams made a poor nailing surface, studs were regularly spaced for that purpose. They were relatively small posts, usually no more than 3 inches square on section. Each was separated from its neighbors by 24 inches on center. Studs were non-weight-bearing and were inserted between the sill and beam with simple joints. Each had to be flush with the outer timber faces of the frame.

FIRST, THE TENON OF THE STUD WAS INSERTED INTO A SILL MORTISE. THEN THE BEVELED TOP WAS SNUGGED INTO A WEDGE-SHAPED SLOT IN THE BEAM. THE SIDES OF THIS MORTISE LAP WERE SAWN ASLANT TO MATCH THE ANGLE OF THE BEVELED STUD END, THEN THE WOOD BETWEEN CHISELED FREE. A NAIL OR TWO AT THE TOP SECURED IT AND THE OTHER STUDS FOR THE OUTSIDE SHEATHING BOARDS AND THE INSIDE PLASTER LATHING.

CLAPBOARD GAUGE

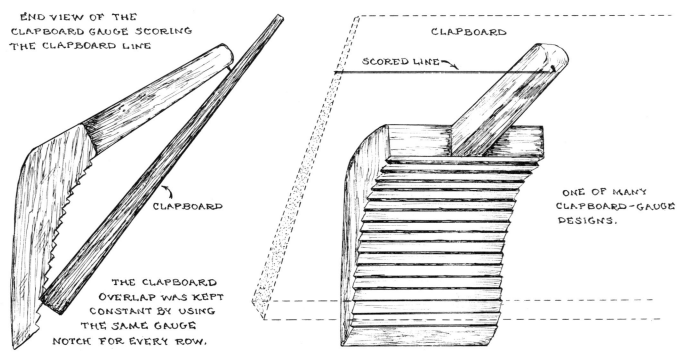

END VIEW OF THE CLAPBOARD GAUGE SCORING THE CLAPBOARD LINE

CLAPBOARD

THE CLAPBOARD OVERLAP WAS KEPT CONSTANT BY USING THE SAME GAUGE NOTCH FOR EVERY ROW.

CLAPBOARD

SCORED LINE

ONE OF MANY CLAPBOARD-GAUGE DESIGNS.

The clapboard gauge scored a line on each clapboard. The bottom edge of each overlapping clapboard was lined up with the scored marks on the previous clapboard row to give the same weather exposure. Nails were then driven in above the scoring, well protected from the elements. The earlier riven oak clapboards of 4 to 6 feet in length were staggered so that no joint was directly above another. The end of each clapboard that joined another was beveled to form a weatherproof joint. Since the rived clapboards were cut the same length as the distances between the centers of the studs, they were nailed together on center with a single nail.

50

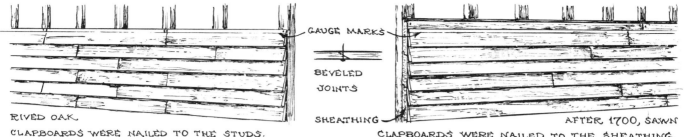

RIVED OAK
CLAPBOARDS WERE NAILED TO THE STUDS.

GAUGE MARKS

BEVELED
JOINTS

SHEATHING

AFTER 1700, SAWN
CLAPBOARDS WERE NAILED TO THE SHEATHING.

By the late 1600s, sawmills were converting raw logs into affordable quantities of boards. Builders began sheathing the entire framework with split and knotty boards that wouldn't do for finish work. The same up-down saws were turning out sawn pine and cedar clapboards in bulk~ and of considerable length. After slicking off the saw marks with the jack plane, the clapboards were set aside until the trim boards for the doors, windows, and corners were in place.

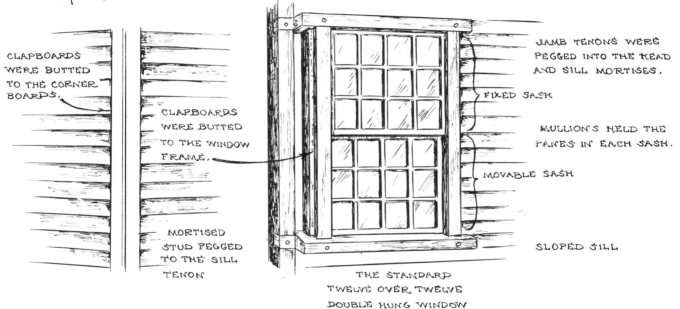

CLAPBOARDS WERE BUTTED TO THE CORNER BOARDS.

CLAPBOARDS WERE BUTTED TO THE WINDOW FRAME.

MORTISED STUD PEGGED TO THE SILL TENON

JAMB TENONS WERE PEGGED INTO THE HEAD AND SILL MORTISES.

FIXED SASH

MULLIONS HELD THE PANES IN EACH SASH.

MOVABLE SASH

SLOPED SILL

THE STANDARD TWELVE OVER TWELVE DOUBLE HUNG WINDOW

Also by the late 1600s, hinged-oak casement windows had been replaced with diamond-shaped panes with double-hung pine window sash. The upper sash was fixed in place, but the lower sash slid up and down, as it does today. Each pane of glass in these double-hung windows measured 6 by 8 inches. This standard size determined the size of the window frame. As a rule, all sashes were four lights or panes wide, however many made up the top-to-bottom length. The earliest windows were eight over twelve (eight lights in the upper sash, twelve in the lower sash or twelve over eight.) It wasn't long before the usual arrangement became twelve over twelve lights for the remainder of the colonial period.

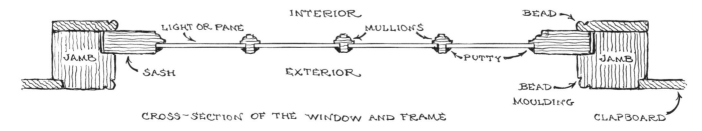

INTERIOR
LIGHT OR PANE
MULLIONS
BEAD
JAMB
SASH
EXTERIOR
PUTTY
JAMB
BEAD
MOULDING
CLAPBOARD

CROSS-SECTION OF THE WINDOW AND FRAME

THE STYLISH GEORGIAN

BEFORE

THE EARLY COLONIAL HOMESTEAD

AFTER

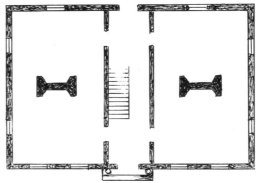

GEORGIAN TWO CHIMNEY BACK-TO-BACK
FIREPLACES

It wasn't that colonial families were dissatisfied with their post and beam homesteads. Certainly the dwellings were rugged, weatherproof, and snug enough. But by 1720, prosperity in the colonies was on the upswing ~ just in time for a more sophisticated architectural style.

Back in England, the Georgian buildings were all the rage. Named for the four kings who began their successive reigns in 1714, the designs did have a touch of royalty. The formal symmetry usually introduced double chimneys and often a hipped roof. Eaves were boxed with fancy moldings. Plain windows were also highlighted with moldings, combinations from the carpenter's planes. Doorways were more outstanding with pediments (triangular caps) and pilasters (rectangular columns with bases and ornamental caps, and set into a wall).

Americans, ever the independent thinkers, often mellowed their Georgian homes with a graceful simplicity that avoided some of the decorative excesses of the new architecture. By the middle of the eighteenth century, these prestigious homes dotted the colonial landscape in considerable numbers.

GEORGIAN DOOR PEDIMENTS
(PAIN, THE BUILDER'S COMPANION, LONDON, 1762)

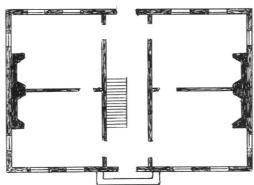

HIPPED ROOF GEORGIAN WITH END WALL HEARTHS

52

The manner of open Pediments with Busto's & Shells for the open part of the *PEDIMENT.*

Compound

Compound

Doric

Ionic

Tympan

COPPER PLATE FROM WILLIAM PAIN'S THE BUILDER'S COMPANION, LONDON, 1762.

53

THE VERSATILE PLANE

Some unsung Roman was the first to tame the chisel into a controlled shaving tool. With the plane, it was possible to copy the classic designs of Rome when the Georgian revival came to our shores. First, the SMOOTHING PLANES cleaned off the humps and bumps in the rough-sawed lumber to give a finished surface bordered by straight and parallel edges. Then the GROOVING PLANES could lock those boards together with dado, tongue and groove, or rebate overlapping cuts. The MOLDING PLANES added their artistry to the cornices, door and window frames, cabinets, and other finishing touches.

WHEN A CHISEL IRON WAS HELD IN A WOODEN BLOCK, THE DEPTH OF THE CUT WAS CONTROLLED.

The plane is the most important tool breakthrough in the past two thousand years. Its many cutting edges have been so useful that the plane is now the most plentiful of all tools and the most prized by collectors. Here follows a bird's-eye look at the colonial plane and its many functions.

SMOOTHING OR BENCH PLANES

Here was the simplest but hardest worker of the plane family. It was little more than a chisel-like iron that was wedged into a slot within a block of wood. When the cutting edge was extended just below the flat sole of a wooden block, a rough board could be shaved smooth and flat.

THE JACK PLANE OR FORE PLANE

SEE MORE ABOUT THE JACK PLANE ON PAGE 49.

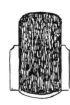

←——— 15" ———→

2½–3-INCH-WIDE CONVEX CUTTING EDGE WITH THE IRON ANGLED AT 45 DEGREES FOR SOFTWOODS AND 50 DEGREES FOR HARDWOODS

JACK PLANES REMOVED LONG AND THICK SHAVINGS FROM ROUGH-SAWN BOARDS. THIS WAS THE FIRST STEP~ AND SOMETIMES THE LAST AS WAS SEEN WITH CLAPBOARDS~ IN THE SMOOTHING PROCESS. OLD-TIMERS CALLED IT THE FORE PLANE BECAUSE IT WAS USED BEFORE ANY OTHERS.

RUN YOUR HAND ACROSS THE UNDERSURFACE OF AN EIGHTEENTH CENTURY DRAWER OR THE BACK BOARDS OF A DESK OR CHEST TO APPRECIATE THE LONG GENTLE SCOOP MARKS.

THE TRYING OR TRUING PLANE

←——— 20" ———→

2½ INCH BLADE WITH SQUARE CUTTING EDGE

THE UNDULATIONS LEFT BY THE JACK PLANE COULD BE "TRUED" UP OR SHAVED FLAT, STRAIGHT, AND PERFECTLY SMOOTH SINCE THE CORNERS OF THE CUTTING EDGE HAD LITTLE OR NO ROUNDING. LONG GROOVES MIGHT SCORE THE WOOD IF THE IRON PROTRUDED TOO MUCH. THE LONG SOLE OF THE PLANE COULD SHAVE THE EDGES OF LENGTHY BOARDS SO STRAIGHT AND TRUE THAT THE BOARDS COULD BE JOINED TOGETHER AS ONE. BECAUSE OF THIS, IT WAS ALSO KNOWN AS A TRUING PLANE.

SMOOTHING PLANE OR COFFIN PLANE

45 TO 50 DEGREES SLANT

6-9"

$1\frac{1}{2}$ TO $2\frac{1}{2}$ INCH CONVEX CUTTING EDGE

OF ALL THE BENCH PLANES, THIS CHUNKY LITTLE COFFIN-OR BOAT-SHAPED PLANE WAS THE MOST POPULAR. ITS CUTTING EDGE WAS SLIGHTLY CONVEX, HALFWAY BETWEEN THE JACK AND THE TRYING-PLANE IRONS, THE SMOOTHING PLANE DID ITS JOB WELL AND COULD PLANE SHORTER LENGTHS THAN THE TRYING PLANE WAS ABLE TO HANDLE. INDEED, IT WAS THE ALL-ROUND GENERAL-USE PLANE ON THE WORKSHOP BENCH. IT, LIKE THE OTHER SMOOTHING PLANES, WAS BEVELED AROUND ITS UPPER EDGES FOR A COMFORTABLE GRASP.

GROOVING PLANES

Grooving planes cleared out excess wood in long square-edged channels along the edges of boards. The narrow stock had a shaving opening that ran side to side. Most of the plane irons had their cutting edges skewed on an angle. Its leading edge drew the blade toward the inner face of the groove. Another distinctive feature of the grooving planes was some sort of guide fence to keep the plane from wandering off its straight and narrow path. (I think there's a moral here somewhere.)

THE DADO GROOVING PLANE

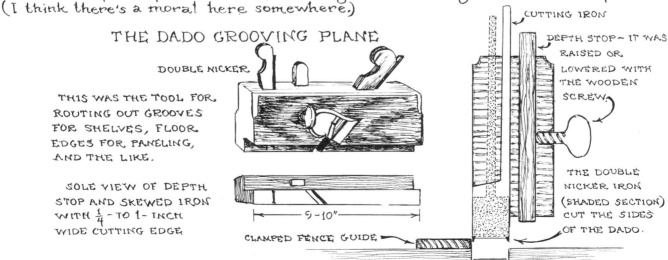

DOUBLE NICKER

CUTTING IRON

DEPTH STOP ~ IT WAS RAISED OR LOWERED WITH THE WOODEN SCREW.

THIS WAS THE TOOL FOR ROUTING OUT GROOVES FOR SHELVES, FLOOR EDGES FOR PANELING, AND THE LIKE.

SOLE VIEW OF DEPTH STOP AND SKEWED IRON WITH $\frac{1}{4}$- TO 1- INCH WIDE CUTTING EDGE

9-10"

CLAMPED FENCE GUIDE

THE DOUBLE NICKER IRON (SHADED SECTION) CUT THE SIDES OF THE DADO.

TONGUE-AND-GROOVE PLANES OR MATCHING PLANES

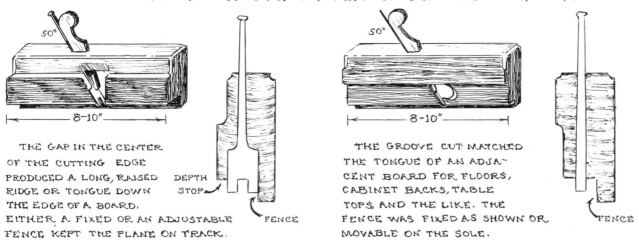

THE GAP IN THE CENTER OF THE CUTTING EDGE PRODUCED A LONG, RAISED RIDGE OR TONGUE DOWN THE EDGE OF A BOARD. EITHER A FIXED OR AN ADJUSTABLE FENCE KEPT THE PLANE ON TRACK.

THE GROOVE CUT MATCHED THE TONGUE OF AN ADJACENT BOARD FOR FLOORS, CABINET BACKS, TABLE TOPS AND THE LIKE. THE FENCE WAS FIXED AS SHOWN OR MOVABLE ON THE SOLE.

REBATE OR RABBET PLANE

THEIR NAME (DEPENDING ON YOUR PRONUNCIATION) CAME FROM THE FRENCH "RABATTRE," TO BEAT DOWN OR REDUCE. WHEN A RECTANGULAR SECTION OR REBATE WAS REMOVED FROM THE CORNER OF A BOARD, IT COULD BE BUTTED TO AND JOINED WITH ANOTHER.

THE REBATE PLANES HAD IN COMMON A CUTTING IRON SLANTED AT FIFTY DEGREES AND WEDGED IN A NARROW STOCK WITH GRACEFUL SHAVING OUTLETS. LIKE THE DADO PLANE, MOST OF THE IRONS WERE SKEWED. MOST REBATE PLANES HAD SOME SORT OF GUIDE FENCE, KNOWN AS A FILLISTER, TO KEEP THE CUT PARALLEL TO THE EDGE OF THE BOARD. THE KIND OF FILLISTER GAVE EACH REBATE PLANE ITS NAME.

COMMON REBATE~

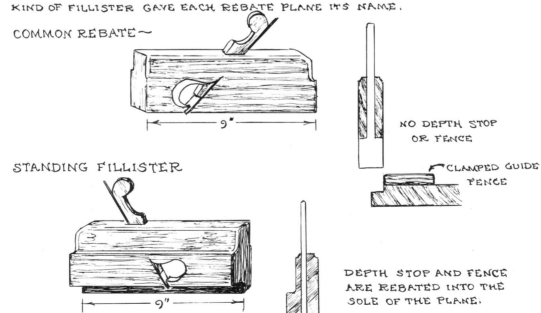

NO DEPTH STOP OR FENCE

CLAMPED GUIDE FENCE

STANDING FILLISTER

DEPTH STOP FENCE

DEPTH STOP AND FENCE ARE REBATED INTO THE SOLE OF THE PLANE.

SKEWED IRON

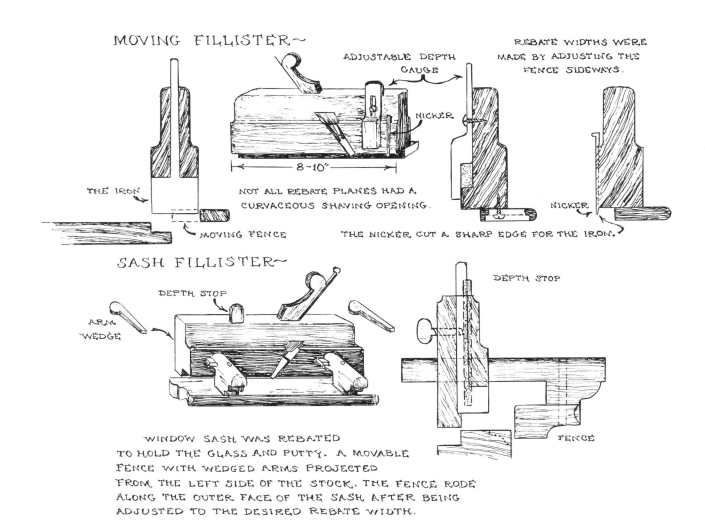

MOVING FILLISTER~

ADJUSTABLE DEPTH GAUGE

REBATE WIDTHS WERE MADE BY ADJUSTING THE FENCE SIDEWAYS.

NICKER

THE IRON

8~10"

NOT ALL REBATE PLANES HAD A CURVACEOUS SHAVING OPENING.

MOVING FENCE

THE NICKER CUT A SHARP EDGE FOR THE IRON.

NICKER

SASH FILLISTER~

DEPTH STOP

ARM WEDGE

DEPTH STOP

FENCE

WINDOW SASH WAS REBATED TO HOLD THE GLASS AND PUTTY. A MOVABLE FENCE WITH WEDGED ARMS PROJECTED FROM THE LEFT SIDE OF THE STOCK. THE FENCE RODE ALONG THE OUTER FACE OF THE SASH AFTER BEING ADJUSTED TO THE DESIRED REBATE WIDTH.

MOLDING PLANES

The molding plane (the English spell it moulding) gave the colonial home a wealth of artistic highlights to otherwise plain wood surfaces. The combinations of curves and angles were as limitless as the woodcrafter's imagination and often gave a local flavor to the Georgian style of architecture. The countless shapes and sizes of the molding cutter blades, especially the large cornice planes, have made them the darlings of tool collectors.

There were three basic types of molding planes. The SIMPLE cutting edges produced such profiles as the hollow and round, cove, and ogee. Combinations of these gave the wide CORNICE molding planes. SPECIAL molding cutters included the chamfer plane and the unique and rare witchet.

SIMPLE

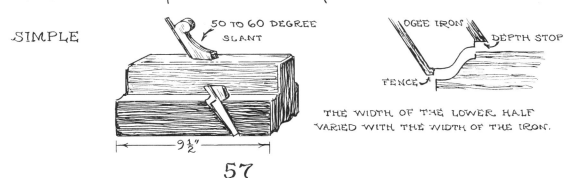

50 TO 60 DEGREE SLANT

OGEE IRON

DEPTH STOP

FENCE

9½"

THE WIDTH OF THE LOWER HALF VARIED WITH THE WIDTH OF THE IRON.

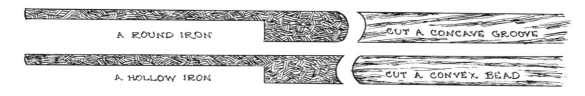

A ROUND IRON — CUT A CONCAVE GROOVE

A HOLLOW IRON — CUT A CONVEX BEAD

MOLDING PLANES WERE KNOWN BY THE PROFILE
EACH PLANED INTO THE WOOD. THE ABOVE HOLLOW
AND ROUND PLANE IRONS WERE THE EXCEPTIONS.

 COVE OGEE FILLET

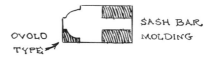 OVOLO TYPE — SASH BAR MOLDING

CORNICE MOLDING PLANES

The cornice plane was the generic name for complex molding planes with many curves and angles. Ranging between 12 and 14 inches in length and 4 to 6 inches in width, it took no little effort to plow the irregular cutting blades into the face of a board. Therefore side handles were needed ~ or a tow rope hole that ran side to side ~ for a helper to pull while the craftsman pushed and guided the plane. The finished work would end up as fancy moldings for eave cornices, chair railings, skirtings, panels, door and window frames, picture frames, furniture trim, and so on.

UNUSUAL MOLDING PLANES

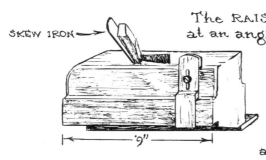

The CHAMFER PLANE shaved a forty-five degree bevel. One leg of the ninety-degree V-shaped sole rode atop the surface of the work. When the other leg of the V contacted the work edge, the chamfer was completed. The depth of the iron's cutting edge determined the size of the bevel.

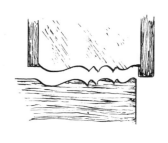

SKEW IRON →

9"

The RAISING PANEL PLANE was held at an angle keeping the adjustable fence horizontal and snug to the board. The depth stop controlled the amount that the panel was raised. The wide sloping panel edge needed a 2-to-4-inch cutting edge set at a skew angle to prevent cross-grain chattering.

DEPTH STOP

FENCE

Moldings for Doors Windows and Chimneys.

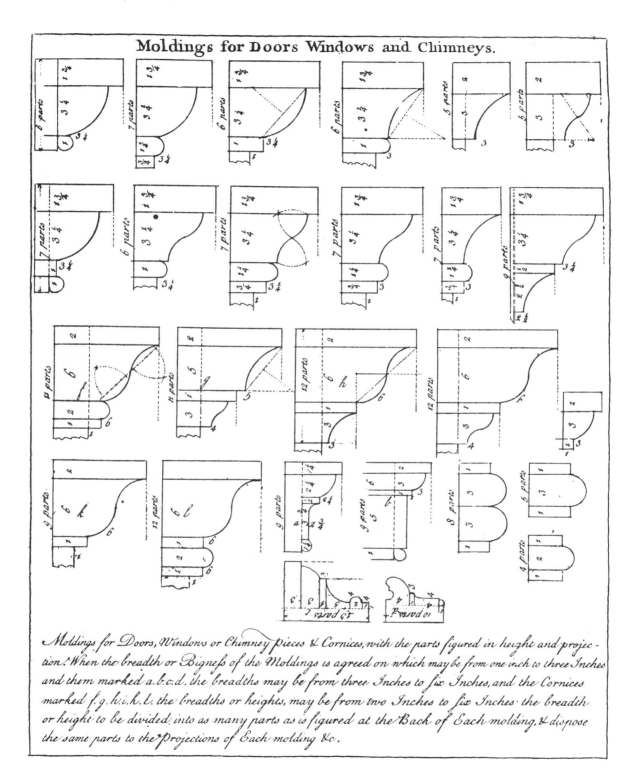

Moldings for Doors, Windows or Chimney pieces & Cornices, with the parts figured in height and projection: When the breadth or Bigness of the Moldings is agreed on which may be from one inch to three Inches and them marked a.b.c.d. the breadths may be from three Inches to six Inches, and the Cornices marked f.g.h.i.k.l. the breadths or heights, may be from two Inches to six Inches· the breadth or height to be divided into as many parts as is figured at the Back of Each molding, & dispose the same parts to the Projections of Each molding &c.

COPPER PLATE FROM WILLIAM PAIN'S *THE BUILDER'S COMPANION*, LONDON, 1762

SHAVING SHORTS

Well after the Revolutionary War, most of the plane-cutting irons were still being shipped from England. Sheffield tools were tops.

The rake of the cutting iron for softwoods~

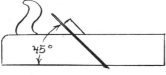

SMOOTHING PLANE

GROOVING PLANE

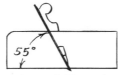

MOLDING PLANE

For hardwoods, the cutting-iron rake was increased five more degrees.

During the last half of the eighteenth century, some smoothing plane cutting irons were joined with a cap iron. This marriage has continued to the present, for the stiffened cutting iron dampened any vibrations. A series of ripples or "chatter" marks were traded for a perfectly smooth surface.

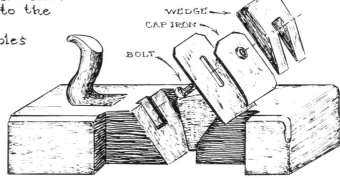

THE "DOUBLE" CUTTING IRON

END GRAIN

Ⓐ   Ⓑ

The cap iron also lifted and broke up the end-grain shavings Ⓑ, thereby preventing a tearing of fibers ahead of the single cutting iron in Ⓐ.

Plane stock was usually of beech or birch. Unlike English and American smoothing planes, the European versions had a wooden horn for the left hand.

Fancy, well-designed makers marks were often embossed on the ends of the plane stock. The owner's stamp was more often ordinary lettering. The fractional numbers on the heels of molding planes indicated the minimal width of the wood needed for planing the molding and not the width of the cutting iron.

GERMAN JACK PLANE

Smoothing plane wedges were broad and beveled. Grooving and molding-plane wedges were thinner and had distinctive notched and rounded heads.

COLONIAL   POST REVOLUTIONARY

To loosen the cutting iron and the wedge, the end grain at the front or the back of the plane was tapped with a wooden mallet~ never an iron hammer. Knocking out the notched head of a grooving or molding plane might be tempting, but sooner or later it would split free. Later nineteenth-century smoothing planes had an end-grain tapping knob at the top front for loosening the wedge without damage.

FRAMING THE PLANED PANEL

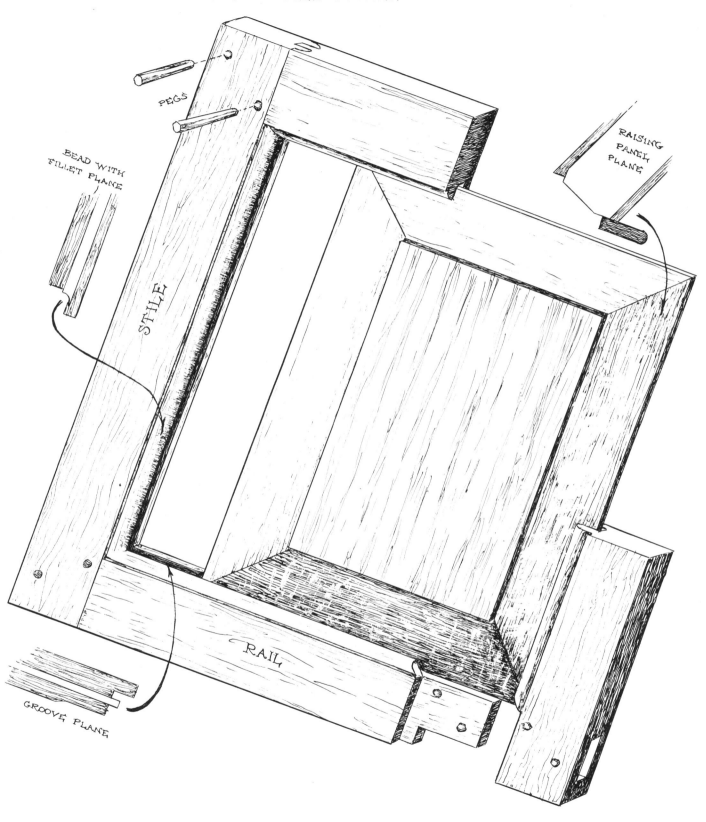

PEGS

BEAD WITH
FILLET PLANE

STILE

RAISING
PANEL
PLANE

RAIL

GROOVE PLANE

61

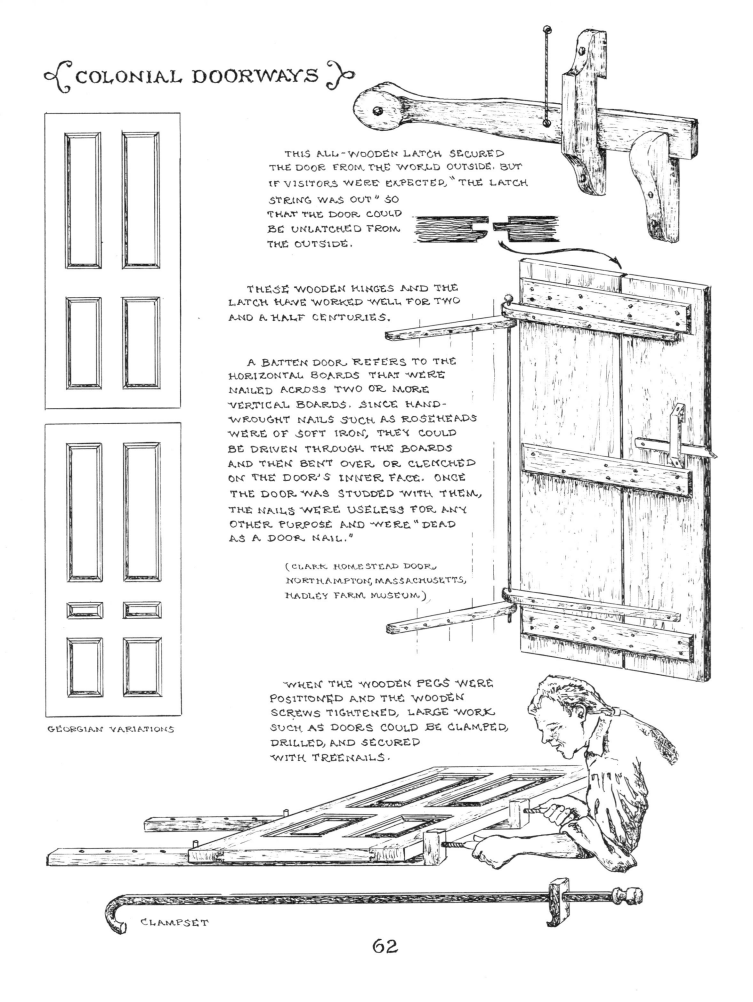

ᘓ COLONIAL DOORWAYS ᘖ

THIS ALL-WOODEN LATCH SECURED THE DOOR FROM THE WORLD OUTSIDE, BUT IF VISITORS WERE EXPECTED, "THE LATCH STRING WAS OUT" SO THAT THE DOOR COULD BE UNLATCHED FROM THE OUTSIDE.

THESE WOODEN HINGES AND THE LATCH HAVE WORKED WELL FOR TWO AND A HALF CENTURIES.

A BATTEN DOOR REFERS TO THE HORIZONTAL BOARDS THAT WERE NAILED ACROSS TWO OR MORE VERTICAL BOARDS. SINCE HAND-WROUGHT NAILS SUCH AS ROSEHEADS WERE OF SOFT IRON, THEY COULD BE DRIVEN THROUGH THE BOARDS AND THEN BENT OVER OR CLENCHED ON THE DOOR'S INNER FACE. ONCE THE DOOR WAS STUDDED WITH THEM, THE NAILS WERE USELESS FOR ANY OTHER PURPOSE AND WERE "DEAD AS A DOOR NAIL."

(CLARK HOMESTEAD DOOR, NORTHAMPTON, MASSACHUSETTS, HADLEY FARM MUSEUM)

GEORGIAN VARIATIONS

WHEN THE WOODEN PEGS WERE POSITIONED AND THE WOODEN SCREWS TIGHTENED, LARGE WORK SUCH AS DOORS COULD BE CLAMPED, DRILLED, AND SECURED WITH TREENAILS.

CLAMPSET

IRONWARE

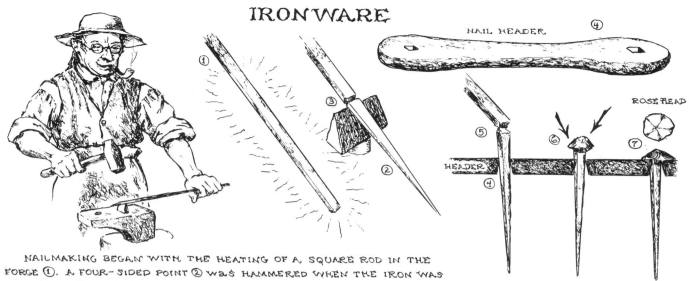

NAILMAKING BEGAN WITH THE HEATING OF A SQUARE ROD IN THE FORGE ①. A FOUR-SIDED POINT ② WAS HAMMERED WHEN THE IRON WAS WHITE-HOT ②. AFTER REHEATING, THE ROD WAS SCORED ON THE TRIANGULAR "HARDY" ON THREE FACES ABOUT HALF AN INCH ABOVE THE HAMMERED SHANK ③. THE STILL HOT ROD WAS THEN INSERTED INTO A "NAIL HEADER" HOLE ④, SNAPPED OFF AND HAMMERED DOWN TO SPREAD THE HEAD. FIVE BLOWS GAVE THE ENGLISH ROSEHEAD WITH FIVE FACES. FRENCH COLONISTS TO THE NORTH FLATTENED THE HEAD WITH THE FIFTH BLOW.

THE "FRENCH HEAD"

Unlike trunnels or wooden pegs, nails didn't grow on trees. Iron was scarce and expensive, and the nails sketched here were highly prized.

THE ROSEHEAD WAS THE COMMON COLONIAL NAIL FOR GENERAL USE.

THE CHISEL POINT WAS WROUGHT ON LARGER NAILS TO PREVENT THIN WOOD SUCH AS SHINGLES FROM BEING SPLIT. WHEN THE CHISEL POINT WAS NAILED ACROSS THE GRAIN, THE PRESSURE WAS WITH, AND NOT ACROSS, THE WOOD FIBERS.

GRAIN

SMALL FLAT-HEADED NAILS TACKED MOLDING TO FURNITURE AND NAILED LATHING STRIPS IN PLACE.

TACKS WERE USED ON LEATHER AND UPHOLSTERY.

T-HEAD

L-HEAD

THE L-HEAD AND THE T-HEAD NAILS HAD HEADS THAT WERE FLATTENED ON TWO SIDES. THEY WERE NAILED WITH THE FLAT SIDES IN THE SAME DIRECTION AS THE GRAIN SO THAT THE HEAD WAS BELOW THE SURFACE OF THE WOOD. THEY SECURED TRIM BOARDS AND ALSO FLOOR BOARDS TO THE JOISTS.

THE CLASP NAIL, WITH ITS SLOPING EDGES, FURTHER ANCHORED THE NAIL INTO THE WOOD.

LARGE FLAT-HEADED NAILS NEEDED A BRAD AWL WITH A CHISEL POINT TO MAKE A PILOT HOLE. IT, LIKE THE CHISEL-POINT NAIL, PREVENTED SPLITTING BY MAKING THE ENTRY SLOT ACROSS THE GRAIN. IT FASTENED DOOR, WINDOW, AND CROWN MOLDINGS IN PLACE.

Cut nails first appeared in America around 1790. By then, Yankee ingenuity had produced a machine that could stamp out nails from sheet iron strips. Because the strip must be turned over to give a complete cut, each side had a rounded and a burred edge. Heads must still be forged as they were in colonial days. Like the iron strap, the iron fibers ran from side to side. They would snap if clinched.

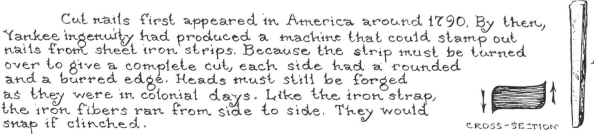

CROSS-SECTION

63

By 1815, it was also possible to punch out a square head on the shank. An indentation just below the head was a by-product of the new technique.

Fifteen years later, the nail machines had enough oomph to chop out a nail with a single stroke. Now both curved edges were along the upper face, and both burred edges on the under face from the downward die cut. They were stronger cut nails, for the iron fibers ran the length of the shank.

1815

1830 ON

Such are the differences between colonial wrought nails and the later cut nails. It might also be mentioned that instead of being pointed, a cut nail acted like a punch, pushing the wood fibers before it. Since there was little side pressure to cause splitting, no brad awl or drill was needed.

HAMMERS

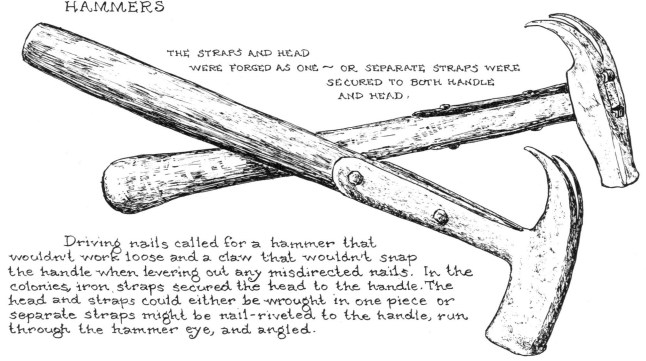

THE STRAPS AND HEAD WERE FORGED AS ONE ~ OR SEPARATE STRAPS WERE SECURED TO BOTH HANDLE AND HEAD.

Driving nails called for a hammer that wouldn't work loose and a claw that wouldn't snap the handle when levering out any misdirected nails. In the colonies, iron straps secured the head to the handle. The head and straps could either be wrought in one piece or separate straps might be nail-riveted to the handle, run through the hammer eye, and angled.

HOUSEHOLD HARDWARE

Although iron nails were an uninspired necessity, there was room for artistic expression when it came to hinges and latches. The blacksmith could combine his own likes and abilities with regional and cultural preferences to produce eye-catching additions for paneled doors.

HINGES

This hardware suspended the door and allowed the lid or shutter to swing freely. Colonial hinges were named for their shapes ~ strap, butterfly, cocks-head, H and H-L hinges. They were usually secured by hand-wrought nails.

NAILED PLATE PINTLES WORKED WELL FOR INTERIOR DOORS.

PINTLE ~ STRAP HINGE ~ EARLY 1600s
BECAUSE THE PINTLE SPIKE REQUIRED A STURDY POST OR A MORTAR BASE, THE HINGE HELD EXTERNAL DOORS.

THIS DUTCH EXAMPLE
SHOWS ONE OF MANY
REGIONAL DIFFERENCES.

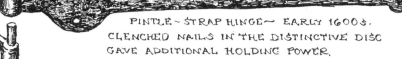

PINTLE~STRAP HINGE~ EARLY 1600$.
CLENCHED NAILS IN THE DISTINCTIVE DISC
GAVE ADDITIONAL HOLDING POWER.

CROSS GARNET STRAP HINGE~ MID~1600$.
AN INSEPARABLE HINGE THAT MUST BE REMOVED TO RELEASE THE DOOR.

A CLOSE COUSIN TO THE CROSS GARNET WAS THE

PLATE AND WRAP~AROUND STRAP HINGE ~ MID~1600s.
THE PLATE SLOT WAS BENT AROUND TO FORM A PIVOTING PIN.

JUST AS TODAY, A PIN
SECURED THE PLATE AND STRAP.

T~HINGE STRAP ~ LATE 1600s.
A LARGE HINGE FOR HEAVY BARN DOORS AND BULKHEADS

WICKET PLATE AND STRAP HINGE ~ LATE 1600s.
A WICKET WAS AN EASY~ACCESS SMALL DOOR CUT INTO A LARGE BARN DOOR.

THE BUTTERFLY HINGE HAD
ITS BEGINNINGS IN THE
1600s AND BY 1700 WAS
HIGH ON THE COLONIALS'
LIST OF FAVORITES.

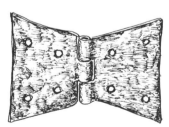

ALTHOUGH NOT STRONG
ENOUGH FOR DOORS,
THE BUTTERFLY WORKED
WELL FOR SMALLER HINGE
DUTY AS CUPBOARD DOORS
AND TRUNK LIDS.

AN AMERICAN
VERSION OF THE
ENGLISH COCKS-
COMB HINGE
IT WAS POPULAR
IN THE 1600s FOR
CUPBOARD DOORS.
LARGER ONES WERE
OCCASIONALLY ON
INTERIOR DOORS.

A MORAVIAN
(PENNSYLVANIA)
COCKSCOMB
1600s

THE H~HINGE WAS
REALLY A SIMPLIFIED
COCKSCOMB. SINCE
THE EARLY 1700s IT
SAW SERVICE AS A
DOOR HINGE.

SINCE THE EARLY 1700s, THE H-L HINGE HAS BEEN ABLE TO CARRY LARGER DOORS THAN THE H HINGE ~ AND ITS L EXTENSION KEEPS THE DOOR FRAME SQUARE.

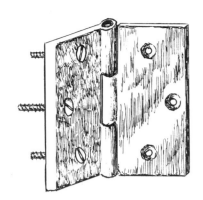

THE HANDSOME WROUGHT HINGES SUDDENLY WENT OUT OF FASHION JUST AFTER THE REVOLUTIONARY WAR ~ ABOUT 1783. THESE CHUNKY CAST-IRON HINGES WERE HELD BY BLUNT-ENDED SCREWS.

SUFFOLK LATCHES

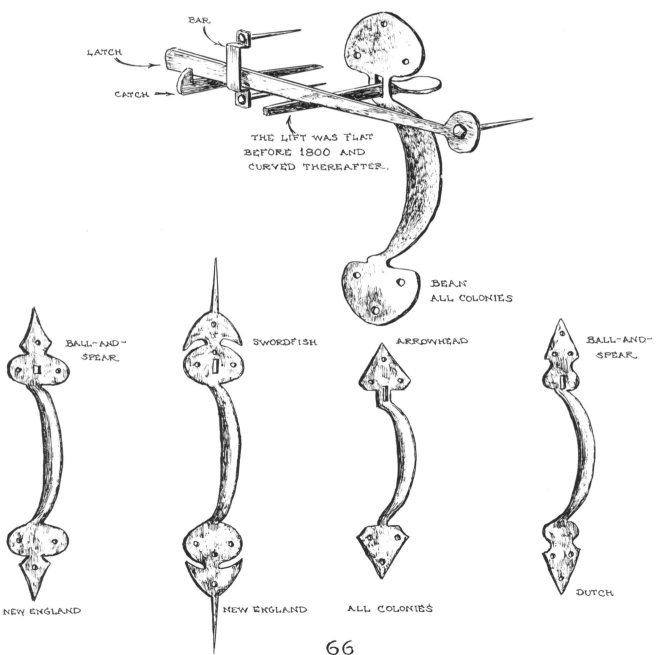

BAR

LATCH

CATCH

THE LIFT WAS FLAT BEFORE 1800 AND CURVED THEREAFTER.

BEAN
ALL COLONIES

BALL-AND-SPEAR

NEW ENGLAND

SWORDFISH

NEW ENGLAND

ARROWHEAD

ALL COLONIES

BALL-AND-SPEAR

DUTCH

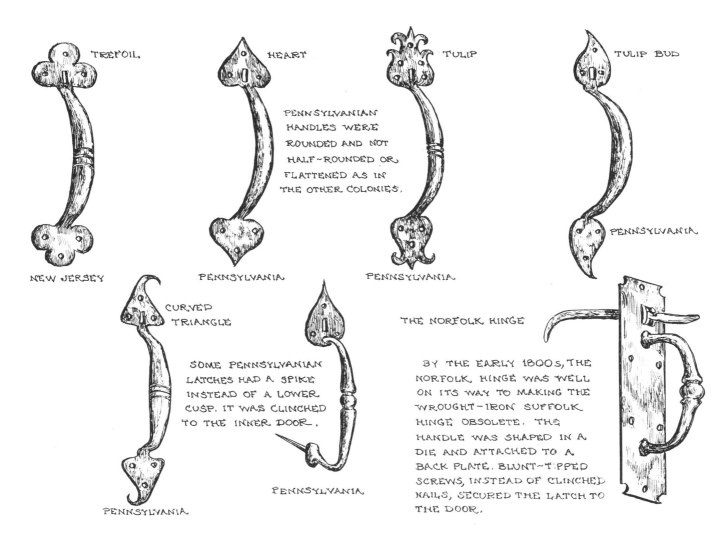

TREFOIL

HEART

TULIP

TULIP BUD

PENNSYLVANIAN HANDLES WERE ROUNDED AND NOT HALF-ROUNDED OR FLATTENED AS IN THE OTHER COLONIES.

PENNSYLVANIA

NEW JERSEY

PENNSYLVANIA

PENNSYLVANIA

CURVED TRIANGLE

THE NORFOLK HINGE

SOME PENNSYLVANIAN LATCHES HAD A SPIKE INSTEAD OF A LOWER CUSP. IT WAS CLINCHED TO THE INNER DOOR.

BY THE EARLY 1800s, THE NORFOLK HINGE WAS WELL ON ITS WAY TO MAKING THE WROUGHT-IRON SUFFOLK HINGE OBSOLETE. THE HANDLE WAS SHAPED IN A DIE AND ATTACHED TO A BACK PLATE. BLUNT-TIPPED SCREWS, INSTEAD OF CLINCHED NAILS, SECURED THE LATCH TO THE DOOR.

PENNSYLVANIA

PENNSYLVANIA

DOOR KNOCKERS

They were the colonial version of a doorbell; they announced the arrival of a visitor.

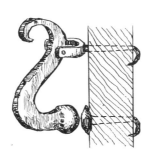

PROTECTING THE HOMESTEAD

Colonial society had its share of bad apples who pursued thievery as a way of life. These sticky-fingered individuals had no use at all for door knockers when they came a-calling. Hooks, hasps, bolts and bars, as well as shutters did what they could to discourage such unwelcome visitations.

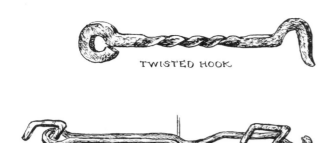

TWISTED HOOK

HOOK WITH RING STAPLE

HASP AND STAPLES

HASP WITH HOOK AND STAPLES

HASP AND HOOK IN STAPLE
PENNSYLVANIA~ MORAVIAN

FOR SOLID SECURITY, THE SLIDING BOLT WAS PREFERRED ABOVE ALL OTHERS. A STOUT
SLIDING OAK BAR KEPT INTRUDERS
AT BAY UNTIL THE 1740s.

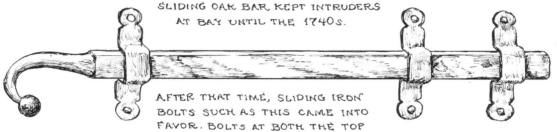

AFTER THAT TIME, SLIDING IRON
BOLTS SUCH AS THIS CAME INTO
FAVOR. BOLTS AT BOTH THE TOP
AND THE BOTTOM OF A DOOR WERE NOT UNCOMMON.

SHUTTERS AND BLINDS

There was comfort in the fact that the doors were well hooked and bolted when the family was away. But windows were an open invitation to smash out a few panes of glass and gain entry. The earliest settlers found that shutters were the answer~ solid battened boards that could be swung closed and "shut up."

In the middle colonies, paired outside shutters were handsome as well as functional additions. Beveled panels were framed by the top and bottom rails and the side stiles.

To the north and south, by the 1750s interior shutters sometimes served the same purpose. These relatively rare paneled shutters either folded at each side of the window opening or slid in a track on the chair rail and the girt at the top of the window.

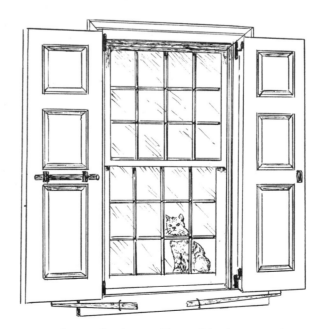

PANELED SHUTTERS ~ PENNSYLVANIA

68

Early blinds had fixed slats between narrow rails and stiles. Used primarily for ventilation, they were closed in the morning when the house was cool. The midday heat was kept out while allowing a shaded light to pass between the slats.

Most authorities feel that blinds didn't appear until after the Revolution. But by the 1850s there were mighty few American homes that didn't take advantage of this air conditioning — including those of colonial vintage. While restoration purists would consider blinds on the pre-Revolutionary home as later additions, they are part of its ongoing history and do give added personality to the exterior.

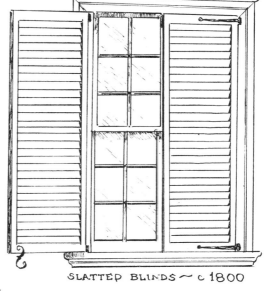

SLATTED BLINDS ~ c 1800

Shutter or blind catches were hand-forged into graceful shapes until the 1790s, when most were cast assembly-line style. Of all the designs, the S-shape catch was far and away the most popular. Each rotated around the cylindrical and headed tenon of a spike. Once the spike had been driven into a clapboard or the mortar of a brick or stone house wall, the catch held the shutter or blind open.

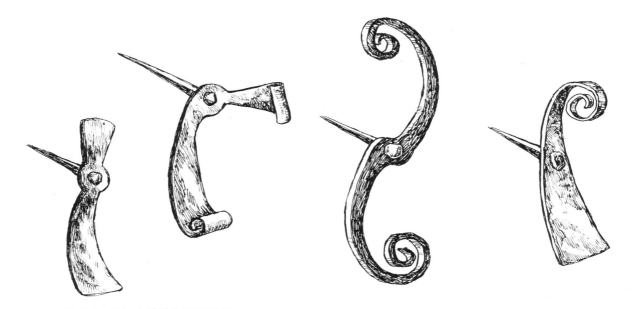

PAINT PROTECTION

From sill to shingles, the post and beam home now had enough wooden armor to ward off centuries of weather. Although paint gave an added exterior shield, most homes were without the expensive coating before the mid-1700s. Thereafter, barn red became a favorite because of its warm color and its low cost iron-oxide pigment. Other popular colors were pumpkin yellow, cream, and white. Doors were highlighted with red, green, blue, or black. A white trim usually set off the other colors to advantage. Paint was worth considering before moving the tools inside for the finish carpentry.

69

FLOORING

Now that the outer shell of the house was weather-worthy the house-wright could turn his attention to the interior work. Temporary planking had served as flooring during the framing process. It was time to replace it with the finish boards that had been seasoning since the first timber was felled. There must be no further shrinkage from drying once the floor boards had been nailed in place.

It wasn't surprising that the English colonists first chose their traditional oak for the floors. Although oak flooring persisted in many kitchens, it was the southern yellow pine and the northern white pine that soon became the woods of choice. These light, durable, and easily worked pines from virgin stands were sawn in random lengths for flooring. Floor boards would range between 10 and 20 inches in width and about an inch in thickness.

HANDSAWS
Parallel chalk lines were snapped on the face of each rough-sawn board, then trimmed with a rip handsaw.

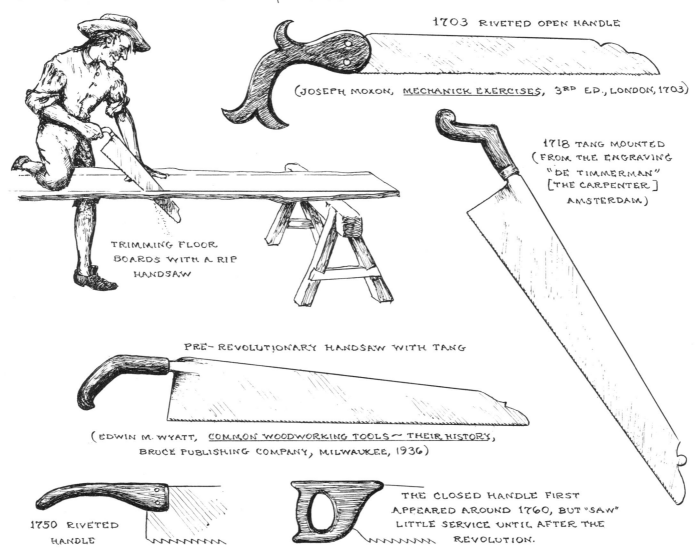

1703 RIVETED OPEN HANDLE

(JOSEPH MOXON, MECHANICK EXERCISES, 3RD ED., LONDON, 1703)

1718 TANG MOUNTED
(FROM THE ENGRAVING "DE TIMMERMAN" [THE CARPENTER] AMSTERDAM)

TRIMMING FLOOR BOARDS WITH A RIP HANDSAW

PRE-REVOLUTIONARY HANDSAW WITH TANG

(EDWIN M. WYATT, COMMON WOODWORKING TOOLS ~ THEIR HISTORY, BRUCE PUBLISHING COMPANY, MILWAUKEE, 1936)

1750 RIVETED HANDLE

THE CLOSED HANDLE FIRST APPEARED AROUND 1760, BUT "SAW" LITTLE SERVICE UNTIL AFTER THE REVOLUTION.

70

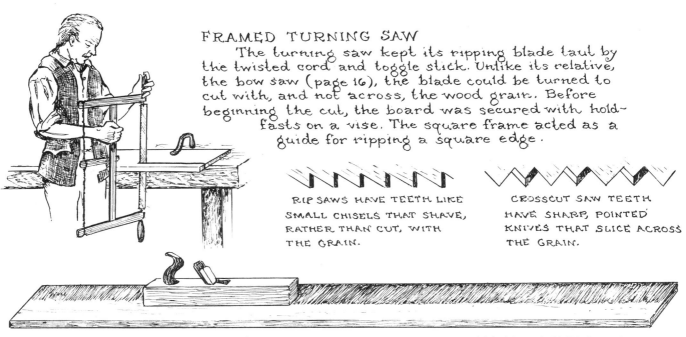

FRAMED TURNING SAW

The turning saw kept its ripping blade taut by the twisted cord and toggle stick. Unlike its relative, the bow saw (page 16), the blade could be turned to cut with, and not across, the wood grain. Before beginning the cut, the board was secured with hold-fasts on a vise. The square frame acted as a guide for ripping a square edge.

RIP SAWS HAVE TEETH LIKE SMALL CHISELS THAT SHAVE, RATHER THAN CUT, WITH THE GRAIN.

CROSSCUT SAW TEETH HAVE SHARP, POINTED KNIVES THAT SLICE ACROSS THE GRAIN.

THE BETTER BOARD FACE WAS THEN PLANED TO A LEVEL SMOOTHNESS WITH A JACK PLANE.

FLOORBOARD JOINTS

To seal any gaps between the floorboards, three edge joinings were used. The fence of the molding plane must rest against the newly planed surface of each squared board.

1. Ship-lap joint

THIS EARLIEST COLONIAL JOINT OVERLAPPED ITS NEIGHBOR BY $\frac{3}{4}$ OF AN INCH. (MOVING FILLISTER PLANE ~ PAGE 57.)

2. Spline or loose-tongue joint

FROM THE EARLY 1700s, THIS JOINING WAS USED IN THE BETTER HOMES. THE $\frac{1}{8}$ - INCH - THICK AND 4 - INCH - LONG WOODEN SPLICE WAS INSERTED INTO GROOVES PLANED INTO THE BOARDS' EDGES.(TONGUE PLANE, PAGE 56.)

3. Tongue-and-groove joint

THIS WAS THE LAST, EASIEST, AND MOST POPULAR JOINT. THE TONGUE, AS WELL AS THE GROOVE, WERE PLANED INTO THE BOARDS' EDGES. (TONGUE AND GROOVE MATCHING PLANES, PAGE 56.)

PREPARATIONS AND PREFERENCES

Most of the temporary floor planking was removed, and a final check of the upper joist surfaces was made. A squared board~ perhaps one of the newly squared floorboards~ was placed on-end across the joists. Humps and valleys would be evident. They would be shaved off with an adz or chocked up to a level surface. Moving the squared board with a level atop its edge will show how successful the joist trimming had been.

71

If the floorboards were pit-sawn, there was an additional step to take before laying. Even the most expert sawyer and his pitman made modest variations in the thickness of each board cut, and a floor with boarding at different levels made a mighty poor walking surface. To make them equal, the width of the thinnest board was scribed along the edges of every thicker board.

SCRIBED LINE

ROUGH PIT-SAWN FACE

It was time for a bit of Yankee know-how. Rather than taking the considerable time and effort to plane the entire rough-cut surface down to a uniform width, the adz could take care of the matter in short order. Wherever a board rested on a joist, the adz could shave off any excess wood down to the scribed lines.

THE MARKING GAUGE SPUR SCRIBED A LINE TO SHOW THE SURPLUS WOOD TO BE REMOVED. THIS JOINING WOULD BE PART OF THE TONGUE AND GROOVE JOINT.

THE ADZED BOARDS WERE TURNED OVER, ROUGH SIDE DOWN, BUT NOT YET NAILED IN PLACE.

THE PIT-SAWN BOARDS, ONCE ADZED AND TURNED OVER, MADE A SINGLE LAYER OF FLOORING. THE SHIP-LAP, SPLINE, OR TONGUE-AND-GROOVE JOINTS PREVENTED CELLAR DRAFTS FROM ENTERING THROUGH ANY GAPS BETWEEN THE BOARDS.

By the middle years of the seventeenth century, any colonial village that was fortunate enough to have a nearby stream would likely have had a sawmill. Precisely cut boardage was being turned out by the wagonload. Now it was possible to have the luxury of a double-boarded first floor, although the second and attic floors continued to be laid as single-layer boards.

72

TONGUE-
AND-GROOVE

OVER THE SUB-
FLOORING WERE THE
SQUARED AND PLANED INCH-
THICK FINISH BOARDS. LAID IN
RANDOM-WIDTH ROWS IN THE SAME
DIRECTION AS THE SUBFLOOR, THE
ENDS OF THE BOARDS BUTTED OVER
A JOIST FOR NAILING. BUTTED ENDS
WERE STAGGERED SO THAT ADJACENT
BOARDS DIDN'T JOIN ON THE SAME JOIST.

THE SUBFLOOR WAS OF POOR QUALITY
BOARDS CALLED "SLIT-STUFF," CUT IN THE SAWMILL
TO A STANDARD HALF INCH THICKNESS, THEY WERE
OFTEN LAID WITHOUT BOTHERING TO SQUARE THE
EDGES, AND ALWAYS ACROSS THE JOISTS AT RIGHT
ANGLES.

SPLINE JOINT

EVERY BOARD TO BE
JOINED MUST BE SNUGGED
CLOSELY TO ITS NEIGHBOR BEFORE
ANY NAILING WAS BEGUN. TWO OR
THREE ROWS OF FLOORING WERE POSITIONED,
BEGINNING AT THE WALL STUDS.

ALONG THE OUTSIDE
ROW, 1-INCH HOLES WERE
DRILLED INTO EVERY OTHER JOIST.
TREENAILS WERE TAPPED INTO THE HOLES.
WOODEN WEDGES WERE DRIVEN BETWEEN THE
PEGS AND THE EDGE OF THE OUTER BOARD.

WHEN WEDGED IN PLACE, THE NAILS
WERE POUNDED HOME. THE L-HEAD
AND THE T-HEAD NAILS WERE NAILED
IN THE SAME DIRECTION AS THE GRAIN
OF THE BOARDS.

The floor was kept clean and
presentable by frequent washings with soap
and then fine sand as an abrasive. Traces of such sand between the floorboards
and the subflooring, found frequently during colonial restorations, was not for
insulation as some have believed. Sometimes a thin layer of the white sand was
left on the floor and swirled into patterns with a broom. It was a second-best
to a rug~ and there were mighty few of those in the early colonies.
     By the mid-1700s, paint had become more available and affordable. Favored
colors for the floors were terra cotta red, pumpkin yellow, gray-green, dark green,
gray, or brown. Spattered paint gave a lively look to the floor, while the more
imaginative householder might have the boards painted to resemble veined marble,
black and white checkerboard, or feature geometric designs. Stenciled floors
were popular following the Revolution and on until 1840.

73

WAINSCOTING

The Dutch "wand schot," meaning "wall protection," may have been its origin. Then again "wain schot," the boarding found in the sides of a wagon, may have been at the root of it. At any rate, our American forefathers considered wainscoting as the sheathing or boarding that formed the walls of a room.

BEFORE 1700

THE FIREPLACE WALL WAS USUALLY COVERED WITH VERTICAL WAINSCOTING, HORIZONTAL BOARDS NAILED NICELY ACROSS THE VERTICAL STUDS.

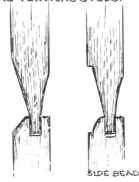

SIMPLE TONGUE AND GROOVE

SIDE BEAD AND RAISED PANEL

Interior walls were sheathed with horizontal or vertical pine boards from the early 1600s. They were joined together with a simple-beveled tongue-and-groove joint. As a wider variety of molding planes became available, the more decorative side bead and raised-panel joint became the moldings of choice. Although fancier joinings followed, the days of the wainscoting were fast fading as the eighteenth century neared.

1700 TO 1725

Prosperity in the colonies spurred on a more elegant wall treatment. Paneling was the answer. A homeowner of some means would likely display a wall of paneling in the front ~ and the most important ~ rooms. Since the fireplace was the focal point for any room, that wall would be the one of choice.

74

It was a short step from sheathing to paneling. The housewright was ready with his assortment of planes that had joined the old wainscoting. A fashionable bead molding gave pleasing highlights and shadows to the framing that surrounded each raised panel. The featured bank of panels was a real testimony to the skill of the craftsmen of that day.

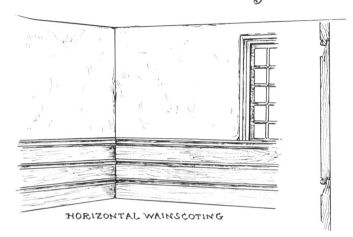

HORIZONTAL WAINSCOTING

The old wainscoting was not forgotten. To compliment the paneled wall, sheathing boards were laid horizontally along the bases of the unpaneled walls. Each was topped by a chair rail~ actually a continuation of the molding that ran under each window sill. Full wainscoting was often retained in the back rooms such as the kitchen and the lesser second floor rooms.

Above the chair-rail wainscoting was a smooth expanse of plaster. It would be white-washed to give a light and airy contrast to the paneled fireplace wall. Paint for the woodwork, although expensive, gave the room a lively, cheerful feeling. By the 1720s, more and more households were using such colors as Indian red, yellow ochre, moss green, and Prussian blue.

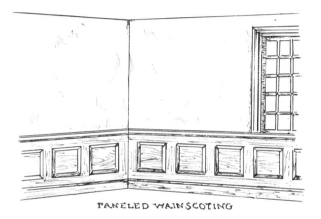

PANELED WAINSCOTING

1725 TO 1775

The older central chimney homes usually had a fireplace wall paneling that was simple and reserved. When the Georgian central-hall and two-chimney home became the style of choice, the front rooms would have a more formal and ornate paneling. The fireplace was flanked by fluted pilasters, pedestals, and caps. A fancy cornice ran along the top of the wall to give an elegant touch.

Paper hangings had become more available and affordable. Printed patterns in the Georgian manner gave a more sophisticated look to the rooms when pasted on the plastered walls. Paneled walls and low wainscoting had seen their day, and by 1800 all that was left of the old wainscoting was the chair rail and baseboard, surrounded by the latest in European wallpaper designs.

75

THE BRACE AND BIT

The auger had been just the tool for boring treenail holes for the great timber-frame joints. But the more refined paneled walls and such interior woodwork called for a more delicate joining.

The brace and bit was the answer. Unlike the hand-switching turns of the auger, the handle of the brace swept around in a continuous circle to give a smooth boring action.

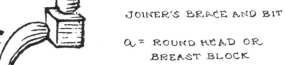

JOINER'S BRACE AND BIT

a = ROUND HEAD OR BREAST BLOCK
b = CHUCK WITH PAD FOR HOLDING THE BIT
c = MAIN BOW OR CRANK
d = CUTTING BIT

DETAIL FROM MOXON, MECHANICK EXERCISES, 3RD ED, LONDON, 1703.

SOME HOMEMADE BRACE HEADS SIMPLY RESTED LOOSELY ATOP THE BOW. PALM PRESSURE KEPT IT IN PLACE AS THE BOW ROTATED.

AMERICAN COLONIAL BRACES WERE GENERALLY MADE BY THE USER. NATIVE HARDWOODS SUCH AS BEECH, MAPLE, CHERRY, AND OAK WERE USED, AND FORTUNATE WAS THE MAN WHO FOUND A CROOKED BRANCH THAT RESEMBLED A BRACE BOW.

THE NATURALLY CURVED AND CONTINUOUS WOOD FIBERS WOULD ADD CONSIDERABLE DURABILITY TO THE TOOL.

THE DIAMETER OF ROTATION SHOULD BE NO MORE THAN 8 INCHES. SINCE A GREATER TURNING FORCE WOULD BE NEEDED, THE WOODEN STOCK MIGHT CRACK.

THESE HANDMADE EXAMPLES MAY BE SEEN AT THE SHELBURNE MUSEUM, SHELBURNE, VERMONT.

FERRULE →

FERRULE →

76

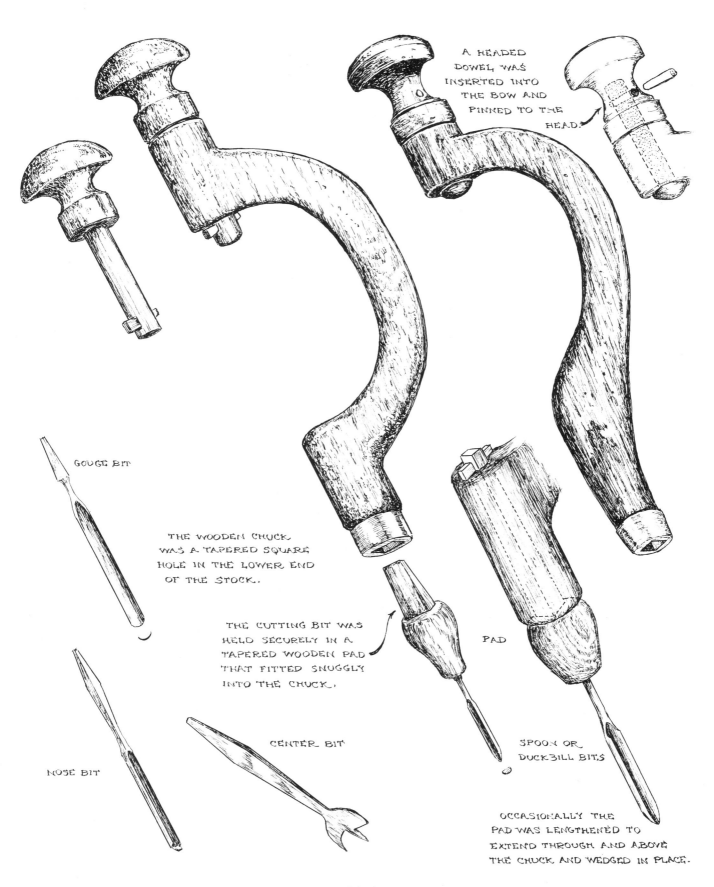

A HEADED DOWEL WAS INSERTED INTO THE BOW AND PINNED TO THE HEAD.

GOUGE BIT

THE WOODEN CHUCK WAS A TAPERED SQUARE HOLE IN THE LOWER END OF THE STOCK.

THE CUTTING BIT WAS HELD SECURELY IN A TAPERED WOODEN PAD THAT FITTED SNUGGLY INTO THE CHUCK.

PAD

NOSE BIT

CENTER BIT

SPOON OR DUCKBILL BITS

OCCASIONALLY THE PAD WAS LENGTHENED TO EXTEND THROUGH AND ABOVE THE CHUCK AND WEDGED IN PLACE.

77

GETTING PLASTERED

When it came to finishing the interior walls of the early seventeenth century, there was an alternative to the vertical and horizontal wainscot boards. Back in Mother England, the few remaining woodlands yielded mighty little boardage. Therefore the gap between the studs was filled with either wattle and daub or bricks. Either provided a surface that was flush to the studs for surfacing with a hay and clay mixture. The studs were first scored to give a holding surface for the thick clay slurry.

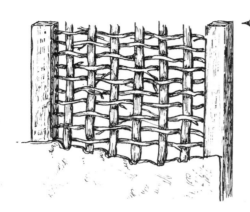

◄ THE ENGLISH WATTLE WAS OF INTERWOVEN BRANCHES THAT FILLED THE SPACES BETWEEN THE STUDS. THE CLAY AND HAY MIXTURE WAS DAUBED ON IN GENEROUS AMOUNTS ON BOTH SIDES OF THE BRANCH FRAMEWORK. THE INNER AND OUTER WALLS BETWEEN THE TIMBERS WERE THEN TROWELED SMOOTH.

THE BRICK FILL WAS LAID ON END AND MORTARED WITH THE MIXTURE OF CLAY AND HAY AS WITH THE WATTLE AND DAUB. THE CLAY MIXTURE WAS SMOOTHED OVER THE STUDS AND BRICKS TO GIVE A FLAT WALL SURFACE. ►

The hay, and later cattle hair served as a reinforcing web of fibers to help prevent cracking or separating from the wall fill.

◄ THE AMERICAN SEVENTEENTH-CENTURY VERSION OF WATTLE AND DAUB CONSISTED OF RIVEN UPRIGHT STICKS OF OAK HELD IN PLACE WITH HORIZONTAL SPLIT BOARDS THAT HAD BEEN SPRUNG INTO STUD GROOVES.

SOME EARLY SEVENTEENTH CENTURY HOMES, MAINLY IN NEW ENGLAND, WERE OF VERTICAL PLANK CONSTRUCTION. HEAVY OAK, UP TO 2 INCHES IN THICKNESS, MADE UP THE OUTER WALLS WITHOUT USING STUDS, THEY WERE PINNED INTO THE RABBETED SILLS. ►

RIVED LATHING WAS NAILED TO THE INNER SURFACES OF THE PLANK WALLS. THE IRREGULAR SPLINTS WERE ENOUGH TO HOLD THE CLAY AND HAY PLASTER.

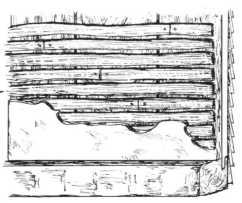

Clay was plentiful in America. When bricks were being made in quantity, they became the wall fill of choice. The outside clapboards were nailed in place before laying up the bricks. (Forest-poor England made do with plaster between the timbers for the exterior as well as the interior walls.) With only clay as mortar, nailing might jar the bricks loose. The plaster was then smoothed over with a trowel.

The old oak lathing came into its own again when the American housewrights began nailing the sticks directly onto the face of the studs. The brick filling was forgotten, and air alone filled the spaces between the studs. After all, brick and plaster had almost no insulation value. The new method proved so popular that most walls ~ and ceilings as well ~ were plastered over riven lathing until 1725.

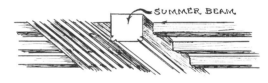

SUMMER BEAM

The walls of the old center-chimney homes could be modernized with a sweep of lathing and plaster. The exposed ceiling joists could be covered in the same way. But updating a ceiling with its massive summer beam projecting well below the joists became something of a head-scratcher. Often the beam was covered with a beaded casing and it was let go at that. After 1750, when the summer beam had faded into history, the end-chimney Georgian featured uninterrupted top-to-bottom plaster.

RIVEN LATHING

The riven-oak lathing strips had also joined the obsolete list. Although each stick had been split off with the grain to make a strong lathing, there was a problem. Each varied from the next in straightness and cross-section. When nailed to the wall studs or ceiling joists, troweling a perfectly flat plaster surface over the lath variations was difficult.

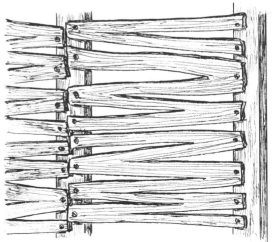

ACCORDION LATHING

The answer was accordion lathing. Its thickness was standardized by sawing boards to the same thickness ~ usually a half an inch. Alternating splits were made partway from each end along the grain. With a gentle pull the splits opened much like an accordion. When nailed in the expanded shape to the wall studs or the ceiling joists, the plaster keyed nicely into the cracks. A final troweling gave a uniformly flat plaster surface.

The accordion lathing was popular for a full century, beginning in 1725. By 1825 laths were sawn by water power on all four sides with identical cross sections.

LATHING TOOLS

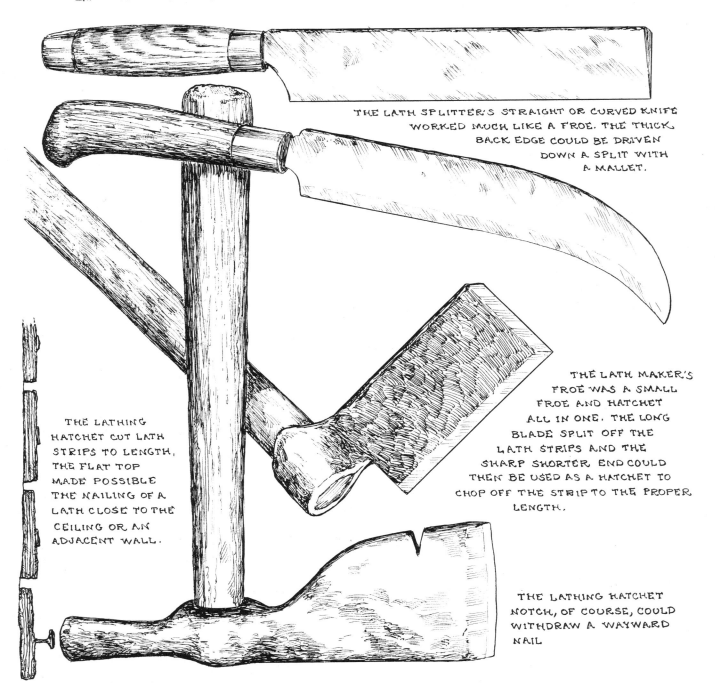

THE LATH SPLITTER'S STRAIGHT OR CURVED KNIFE WORKED MUCH LIKE A FROE. THE THICK BACK EDGE COULD BE DRIVEN DOWN A SPLIT WITH A MALLET.

THE LATHING HATCHET CUT LATH STRIPS TO LENGTH, THE FLAT TOP MADE POSSIBLE THE NAILING OF A LATH CLOSE TO THE CEILING OR AN ADJACENT WALL.

THE LATH MAKER'S FROE WAS A SMALL FROE AND HATCHET ALL IN ONE. THE LONG BLADE SPLIT OFF THE LATH STRIPS AND THE SHARP SHORTER END COULD THEN BE USED AS A HATCHET TO CHOP OFF THE STRIP TO THE PROPER LENGTH.

THE LATHING HATCHET NOTCH, OF COURSE, COULD WITHDRAW A WAYWARD NAIL

80

LIME PLASTER

Clay was inexpensive and plastic enough to fill the voids between bricks or stones, yet it lacked the permanence of lime mortar when exposed to the elements. Many brick and stone chimneys were laid with clay up to the shingles, but above that only the weather-worthy lime mortar would do. Judge Samuel Sewall's diary gave a case-in-point when he wrote of a Massachusetts calamity: " October 30, 1630, a stone house which the governor was erecting at Mystic was washed down to the ground in a violent storm, the walls being laid in clay instead of lime." *

While the stonelike lime mortar and plaster made clay a second best, the raw materials were not always at hand. Fortunate were those colonial areas that could dig up local deposits of limestone or marble. All along the Atlantic shoreline were ancient Indian shell mounds that yielded a bonanza in lime. (Back in England, chalk deposits served the same purpose for filling in the wall spaces in the half-timbered homes.) The raw lime (calcium carbonate) harvest was then processed into a moisture-resistant covering over the lath framework.

KILNS

After "burning" the lime (calcium carbonate) for several days, carbon dioxide was driven off to leave quicklime (calcium oxide).

UPPER LAYER OF LIME

LOWER LAYER OF FIREWOOD

SUCCESSIVE LAYERS OF LIME AND FIREWOOD WERE LAID IN FROM THE TOP.

THROUGH THE GAPS IN AN INNER DOME OF STONES, THE FIRE COULD BE STARTED FROM BELOW AND THE QUICKLIME COULD DROP THROUGH AFTER BURNING.

LIME

LIME

LIME

QUICKLIME

(CONJECTURAL)

THIS MAKE-DO KILN HAD A CENTER HOLE THROUGH THE LAYER OF RADIALLY-STACKED FIREWOOD AND A LESSER LAYER OF LIME. THE KILN WAS FIRED BY DROPPING LIT TINDER DOWN THE HOLE, BURNING THE FIREWOOD OUTWARD AND UPWARD FROM THE INSIDE. *

-KILN OF STONEWORK OR BRICK-
A WOODEN COVER OVER THE BOTTOM OPENING CONTROLLED THE DRAFT AND THE BURNING RATE. AFTER COOLING, THE COVER WAS REMOVED TO SHOVEL OUT THE QUICKLIME. *

~ THE CHEMICAL REACTION ~

$$CaCO_3 + 1650 \text{ DEGREES F.} \rightarrow CaO + CO_2$$

LIME
(CALCIUM CARBONATE)

QUICKLIME
(CALCIUM OXIDE)

CARBON DIOXIDE

The shape of the fist-sized lumps of limestone or marble and the shells of the oyster or other shellfish appeared unchanged. After being removed from the kiln, the quicklime pieces were cleaned of ashes and char. Then came a problem. If quicklime was exposed to the air over time, carbon dioxide would rejoin the quicklime and revert to the inert lime. Or moisture might be absorbed, and partially convert the quicklime to portions of hydrated or slaked lime. The solution was to add a measured amount of water to the pieces of quicklime shortly after the removal from the kiln ~ with rather startling results.

* McKEE, INTRODUCTION TO EARLY AMERICAN MASONRY, NATIONAL TRUST FOR HISTORIC PRESERVATION, 1973.

THE BODIES OF THOSE WHO DIED ON THE BATTLE FIELD OR OF A CONTAGEOUS DISEASE WERE SOMETIMES SPRINKLED WITH QUICKLIME TO HASTEN DEHYDRATION AND DECOMPOSITION OF THE TISSUES.

$$CaO \quad + \quad H_2O \longrightarrow Ca(OH)_2$$

QUICKLIME   WATER   SLAKED OR HYDRATED LIME

(CALCIUM OXIDE)   (CALCIUM HYDROXIDE)

A violent eruption of steam and heat erupted as the quicklime (calcium oxide) was sprinkled with a predetermined amount of water. Shortly the stone chunks or shells cracked and then became a fine white powder of slaked or hydrated lime (calcium hydroxide). More water was added and let stand in a container for several days. This prevented any unslaked pieces from later expanding from delayed hydration, thereby cracking off pieces of finished plaster. Then the lime paste was ready for sand and hair to be added.

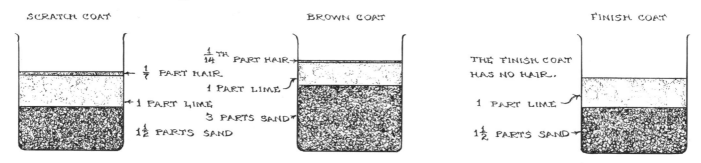

SCRATCH COAT

$\frac{1}{7}$ PART HAIR

1 PART LIME

$1\frac{1}{2}$ PARTS SAND

BROWN COAT

$\frac{1}{14}$ TH PART HAIR

1 PART LIME

3 PARTS SAND

FINISH COAT

THE FINISH COAT HAS NO HAIR.

1 PART LIME

$1\frac{1}{2}$ PARTS SAND

PLASTERING TOOLS

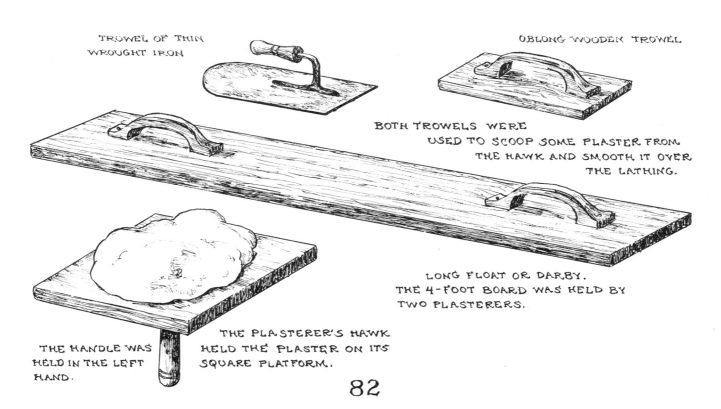

TROWEL OF THIN WROUGHT IRON

OBLONG WOODEN TROWEL

BOTH TROWELS WERE USED TO SCOOP SOME PLASTER FROM THE HAWK AND SMOOTH IT OVER THE LATHING.

LONG FLOAT OR DARBY. THE 4-FOOT BOARD WAS HELD BY TWO PLASTERERS.

THE HANDLE WAS HELD IN THE LEFT HAND.

THE PLASTERER'S HAWK HELD THE PLASTER ON ITS SQUARE PLATFORM.

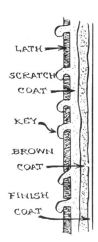

LATH →

SCRATCH
COAT →

KEY →

BROWN
COAT →

FINISH
COAT →

Like mud being squeezed between a child's fingers, the scratch coat was trowel-pressured into the lathing splits. The blobs that oozed down behind the laths were keys that gave a tenacious grip when dry. Over this was troweled the brown coat, tinted with its rich mixture of sand and hair. The finish coat, containing more lime and no hair, was smoothed on like icing on a cake.

A few minor irregularities might be noticed after the plaster layers had set. The early rived lath could give a waviness to the plaster surface. Since the split laths absorbed moisture from the plaster, some slight bulging might show between the studs. Even so, there was a handcrafted charm that was lost when laths were sawn straight on all sides.

LATH SEPARATIONS SHOULD BE WIDE ENOUGH TO FORM THE KEY RIDGES IF A MODERN PENCIL CAN FIT BETWEEN THE SPACES.

Owners of less imposing homes usually whitewashed their plastered walls and let it go at that. (Whitewash was nothing more than brushed-on quicklime slaked in water.) For those with more jingle in their pockets, imported wallpapers gave the Georgian home a touch of elegance. Yellow, green, blue, and gray for the interior woodwork complimented the paper. An added touch might be a "landskip," painted by an itinerant artist on a panel over the fireplace.

STAIRS

The decades had seen radical changes in the treatment of interior walls ranging from wainscot to paneling and then on to plaster. Meanwhile staircases kept pace with the times to complement the updated walls.

BEFORE 1700

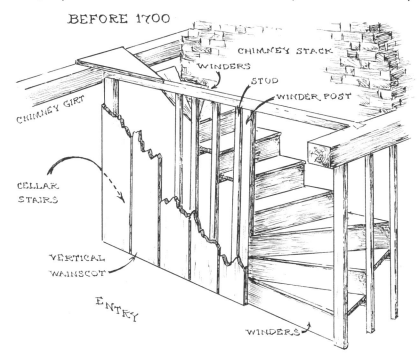

CHIMNEY STACK

WINDERS

STUD

WINDER POST

CHIMNEY GIRT

CELLAR STAIRS

VERTICAL WAINSCOT

ENTRY

WINDERS

In the earlier colonial homes, space was at a premium. This was especially true of the central-chimney home. The great fireplace stack had crowded the entry hall and stairway into a short, narrow space. Of necessity, the angle of ascent was steep with risers and narrow treads. Winders, those pie-shaped stops that were framed in and pivoted around a square oak post, were real space savers. The straight run of steps was supported by the studs that also held the enclosing vertical wainscoting. There were no handrails.

83

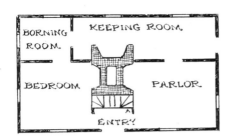

FLOOR PLAN FOR A
CENTRAL CHIMNEY HOUSE

BORNING ROOM | KEEPING ROOM
BEDROOM | PARLOR
ENTRY

1700 TO 1725

EARLY PERIOD STAIRS

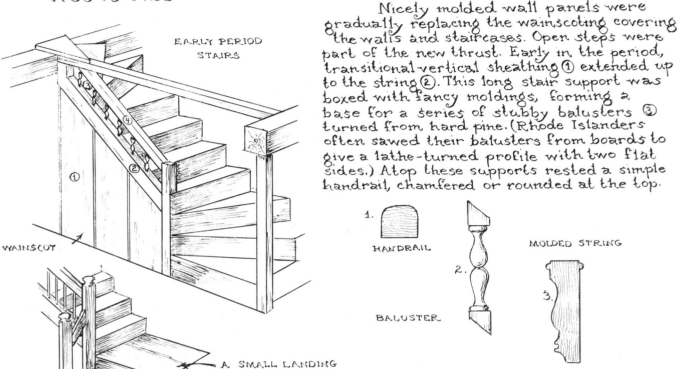

WAINSCOT

A SMALL LANDING
COULD BE USED IN
PLACE OF WINDERS

Nicely molded wall panels were gradually replacing the wainscoting covering the walls and staircases. Open steps were part of the new thrust. Early in the period, transitional vertical sheathing ① extended up to the string ②. This long stair support was boxed with fancy moldings, forming a base for a series of stubby balusters ③ turned from hard pine. (Rhode Islanders often sawed their balusters from boards to give a lathe-turned profile with two flat sides.) Atop these supports rested a simple handrail, chamfered or rounded at the top.

1.

HANDRAIL

2.

BALUSTER

MOLDED STRING

3.

As the period progressed, the short balusters were lengthened into more graceful turnings ④. The handrail was embellished with moldings on the outer face ⑤, giving an asymmetrical cross-section. Newel posts were often turned on a lathe, including a cap of sorts at the top ⑥. Occasionally the supporting post at the top of the stairs was extended below the ceiling as a decorative feature ⑦.

5.

4

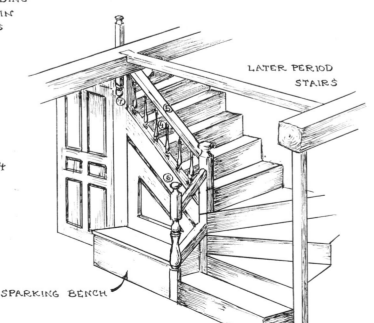

LATER PERIOD STAIRS

SPARKING BENCH

Sparking benches~ certainly the stairs of the central chimney were a bit cramped, but they did have an advantage over the straight-run stairs of the middle and southern colonies. There was just space enough against the paneled wainscot of the entry stairs for a small seat. Tradition has it that after calling on one's best girlfriend, there were a few moments to linger before the last goodnights. It was a tight fit for a couple making sparks, but history has never recorded any complaints.

BOXED-STRING CONSTRUCTION

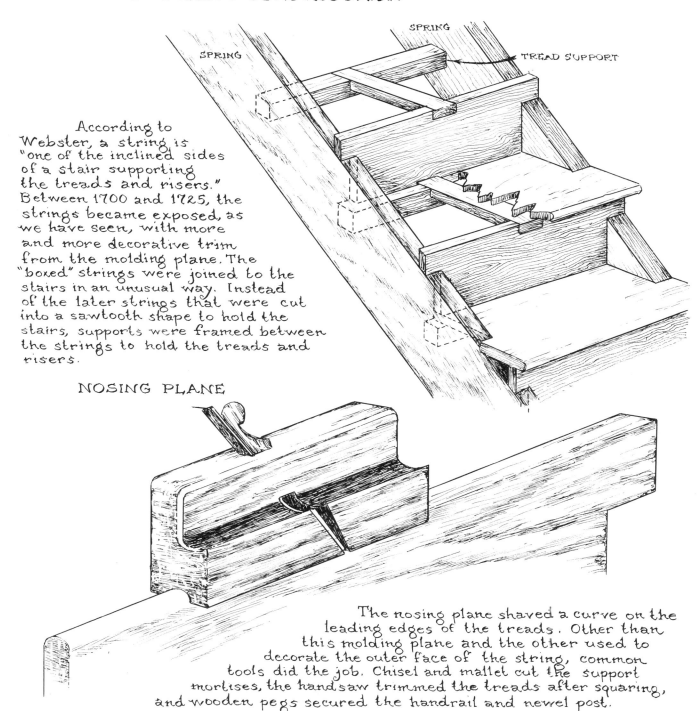

SPRING

SPRING

TREAD SUPPORT

According to Webster, a string is "one of the inclined sides of a stair supporting the treads and risers." Between 1700 and 1725, the strings became exposed, as we have seen, with more and more decorative trim from the molding plane. The "boxed" strings were joined to the stairs in an unusual way. Instead of the later strings that were cut into a sawtooth shape to hold the stairs, supports were framed between the strings to hold the treads and risers.

NOSING PLANE

The nosing plane shaved a curve on the leading edges of the treads. Other than this molding plane and the other used to decorate the outer face of the string, common tools did the job. Chisel and mallet cut the support mortises, the handsaw trimmed the treads after squaring, and wooden pegs secured the handrail and newel post.

85

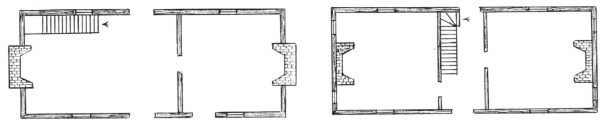

CHIMNEY AND STAIR LOCATIONS IN SOUTHERN HOMES 1725 TO 1775

THE GEORGIAN STAIRCASE

The Georgian style came as a welcome change. Two chimneys several feet from the gables took the place of the single central-chimney stack in the more northerly colonies. In the warmer south, where chimneys could be located within or extend outward from the gabled ends, the interior alterations were less drastic. The result was an open and airy central hall with plenty of elbow room. Now the very visible staircase took on added importance.

Among the striking changes was a longer, more gradual angle of ascent with wider treads and lower risers. The earlier boxed or closed strings became open strings with the ends of the treads showing. Scroll-shaped brackets secured the treads to the strings. Well-turned balusters marched up the run like so many soldiers, with three secured to each tread. Often there were alternating patterns of spiral or gracefully turned forms. The newel post, not to be outdone, was set out beyond the handrail line placing its many turning and carvings on notice. A welcoming handrail curved out to rest on the newel post. All in all, the staircase was now an important architectural feature worthy of the prospering colonies.

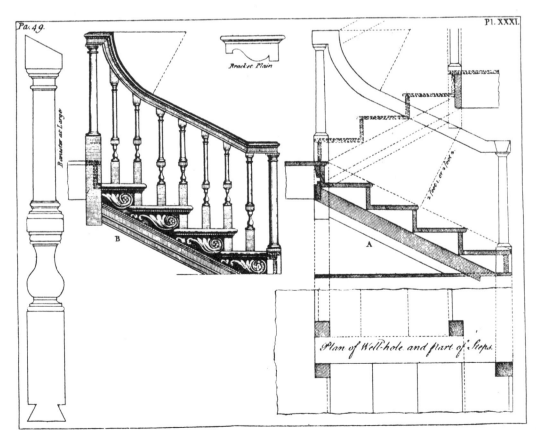

{ To face PLATE 31. }

Plate 31 ſhews the Section and Elevation of Stairs, with the Method of fixing the Strings, Rails, and Newels for the Steps; alſo the Method of ſtriking the Ramps, Knees, &c. in a plain and eaſy Manner, with the Well-hole, and Plan of the Stairs, the Height of the Rails, Baniſters, Newels, &c. which, by Inſpection, will appear ſo plain as to need no further Explanation.

Plate 32 is a Plan of the Hand-Rail, and circular Cap, ſhewing the Mitre of the Rail to the circular Cap on the Newel, and a Cap for Iron Hand Rail, &c.

A the Section of the Stairs, B the Elevation.

To draw the Plan and Scrole of a twiſt Rail for a Staircaſe.

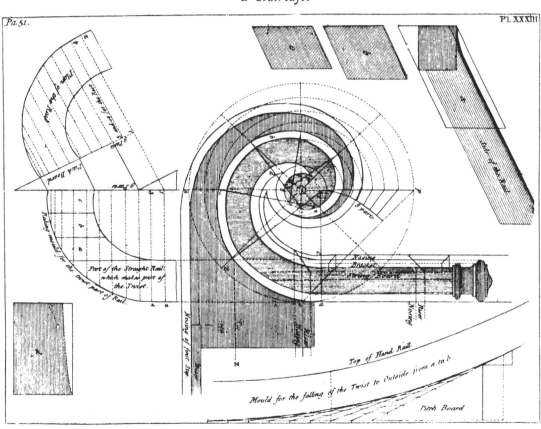

PLATE XXXI WITH EXPLANATION AND PLATE XXXIII ARE FROM WILLIAM PAIN'S THE BUILDER'S POCKET-TREASURE, ENGRAVED BY ISAAC TAYLOR, LONDON, W. OWEN, 1763.

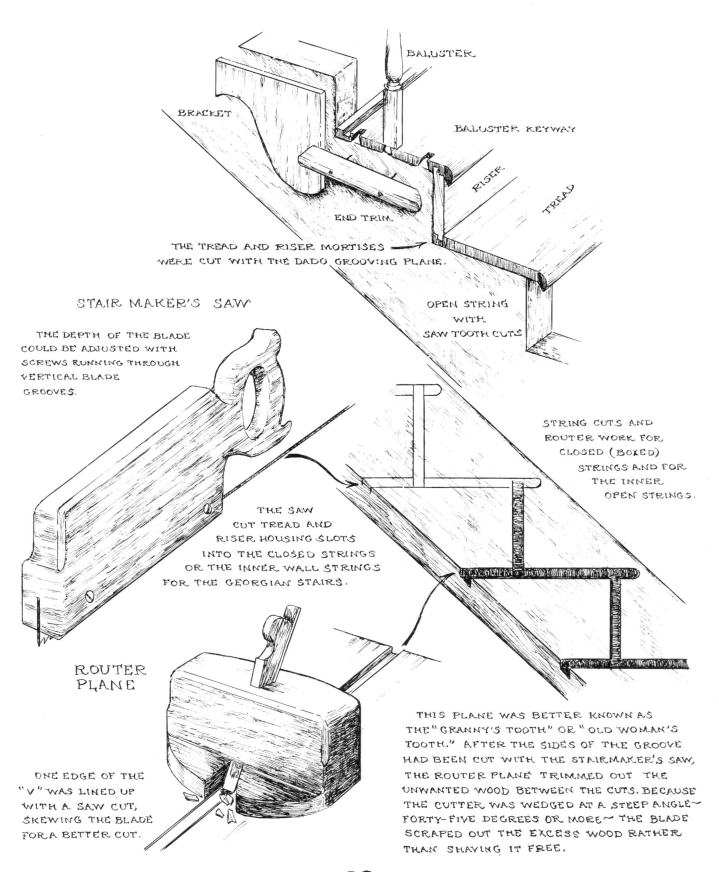

BALUSTER

BRACKET

BALUSTER KEYWAY

RISER

TREAD

END TRIM

THE TREAD AND RISER MORTISES
WERE CUT WITH THE DADO GROOVING PLANE.

OPEN STRING
WITH
SAW TOOTH CUTS

STAIR MAKER'S SAW

THE DEPTH OF THE BLADE
COULD BE ADJUSTED WITH
SCREWS RUNNING THROUGH
VERTICAL BLADE
GROOVES.

STRING CUTS AND
ROUTER WORK FOR
CLOSED (BOXED)
STRINGS AND FOR
THE INNER
OPEN STRINGS.

THE SAW
CUT TREAD AND
RISER HOUSING SLOTS
INTO THE CLOSED STRINGS
OR THE INNER WALL STRINGS
FOR THE GEORGIAN STAIRS.

ROUTER
PLANE

ONE EDGE OF THE
"V" WAS LINED UP
WITH A SAW CUT,
SKEWING THE BLADE
FOR A BETTER CUT.

THIS PLANE WAS BETTER KNOWN AS
THE "GRANNY'S TOOTH" OR "OLD WOMAN'S
TOOTH." AFTER THE SIDES OF THE GROOVE
HAD BEEN CUT WITH THE STAIRMAKER'S SAW,
THE ROUTER PLANE TRIMMED OUT THE
UNWANTED WOOD BETWEEN THE CUTS. BECAUSE
THE CUTTER WAS WEDGED AT A STEEP ANGLE~
FORTY-FIVE DEGREES OR MORE~ THE BLADE
SCRAPED OUT THE EXCESS WOOD RATHER
THAN SHAVING IT FREE.

Other tools helpful in staircase construction were:

MITER BOX AND SAW

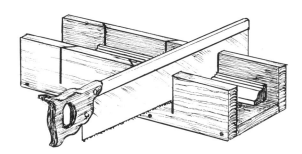 CROSSCUT

TURNING SAW (FRETWORK)

CROSSCUT

The miter box was made of three hardwood boards with forty-five-and ninety-degree angles sawn down to the baseboard. The box was usually secured to the benchtop or held in a vise.

The miter saw was a crosscut backsaw, stiffened along its back with a brass or a wrought-iron sleeve. Its rectangular blade had enough width to keep the back above the top edges of the miter box. With the molding or board to be cut held firmly against the back board of the box, accurate angles were made when sawing on the horizontal. The combination is still a useful addition in the workshops of today.

Framed saws had a problem. As the depth of the cut increased, the stretcher would crowd into the edge of the work. Framed turning saws were the answer. The blade could be "turned" in any direction by twisting the two connecting handles. Of course equal twists were necessary to prevent a spiraling of the blade. In this way the sturdy rip-saw version was distanced from the edge of the board when ripping with the grain (see page 71).

A more delicate version was the framed fine-bladed crosscut or fretwork saw. The blade wasn't much more than a foot in length admirably suited for cutting fancy scrolls and designs such as the stair brackets. The turning handles gave clearance for the stretcher as the blade curved its way through the work.

STAIRBUILDER'S PLANES

SHELBURNE MUSEUM,
SHELBURNE,
VERMONT

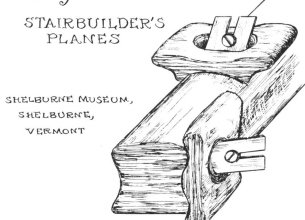

HANDRAIL SHAVE

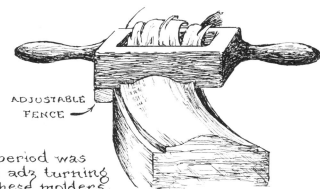

ADJUSTABLE FENCE ⟵

The curved handrail of the Georgian period was first rough-shaped with such tools as the adz turning saw, and drawshave, then finished with these molders.

WORKBENCH HOLDING TOOLS

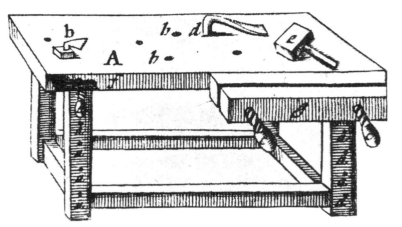

MOXON, MECHANICK EXERCISES, 3RD ED., LONDON, 1703.

MOXON'S PLATE 4 PAGE 69

(A) WORKBENCH
(b) CATCH OR STOP
(bb) HOLES FOR SECURING THE CATCH, HOLDFAST, OR PEGS
(c) MALLET FOR SETTING OR LOOSENING THE HOLDFAST
(d) HOLDFAST
(f) SMALL ONE SCREW VISE (POORLY DEFINED)
(8) VISE
(aa AND dd) PEG HOLES FOR HOLDING VERTICAL BOARDS

VOLUME 7 "MENUSIE"

(A) HOLDFAST
(B) HOLDFAST HOLES IN BENCHTOP
(C) PEG HOLES IN LEGS TO SUPPORT VERTICAL BOARDS
(G) TOP BENCH CLAMP
(K) WEDGE (SHOULD BE AT FAR LEFT CORNER) TO HOLD A VERTICAL BOARD WHILE SUPPORTED BY PEGS IN THE PEG HOLES IN LEGS (C)

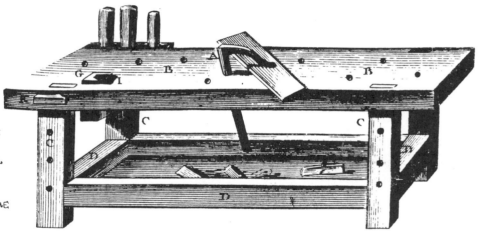

DIDEROT, RECUEIL DE PLANCHES SUR LES SCIENCES ET LES ARTS LIBÉRAUX, PARIS, 1769.

These eighteenth-century workbenches, with their tops at comfortable waist-high working level, bristle with all manner of holding tools. Much like an extra pair of hands, they gripped the work to free the craftsman for the exacting work at hand. Planing, sawing, chiseling, carving, and mortising of finish exterior or interior work such as the fancy Georgian staircases made the workbench and its holding tools a must.

CATCH OR STOP

When planing the broad surface of a board, catches were dropped into a series of bored bench holes to prevent any shifting of the work. Two catches were inserted at one end of the board and three were positioned along the long edge opposite to the planer.

90

Catches rested well below the surface of the board to give an unobstructed planing surface. Since the teeth of the wrought-iron catches might scar any newly planed edges and ends of the wood, wooden pegs could be substuted.

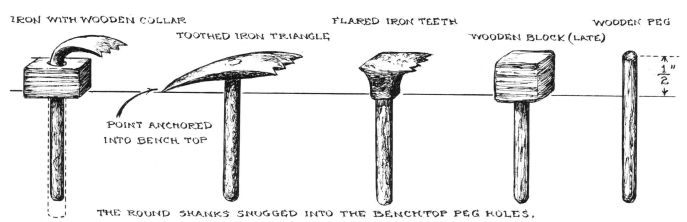

IRON WITH WOODEN COLLAR

TOOTHED IRON TRIANGLE

FLARED IRON TEETH

WOODEN BLOCK (LATE)

WOODEN PEG

POINT ANCHORED INTO BENCH TOP

$\frac{1}{2}$"

THE ROUND SHANKS SNUGGED INTO THE BENCHTOP PEG HOLES.

TOP BENCH CLAMP

This simplest of clamps was nothing more than a $\frac{3}{4}$-inch board about 4 inches wide and 8 inches long, with a thirty-degree notch. The end of an upright board was wedged into the notch, ready for its upper edge to be planed.

THE CLAMP WAS NAILED IN THE CORNER OF THE BENCH.

EASILY MADE, THE CLAMP IS USEFUL IN TODAY'S WORKSHOP.

HOLDFAST

The shank of the all-iron holdfast was first placed in a larger diameter hole in the top of the workbench. The board to be worked was positioned under the arm pad — or separated from it by a piece of scrap wood to prevent scarring of the work.

A light tap ① wedged the shank into the bench hole to hold the board fast. To loosen, the shank was tapped ② toward the iron arm pad.

Because the arm and pad interfered with surface planing, the holdfast was better used for mortising, chiseling, carving, and the like.

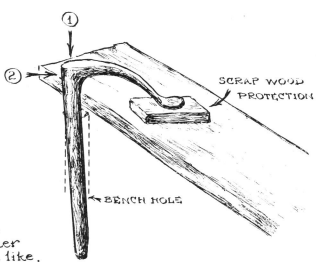

SCRAP WOOD PROTECTION

BENCH HOLE

91

SIDE REST

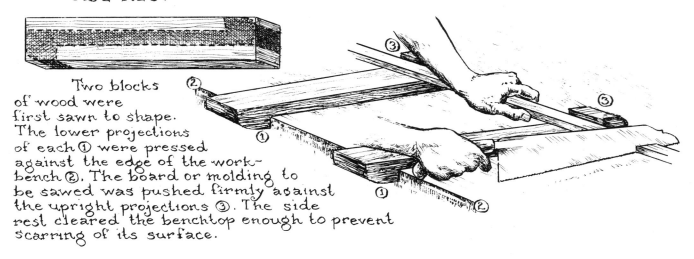

Two blocks of wood were first sawn to shape. The lower projections of each ① were pressed against the edge of the work-bench ②. The board or molding to be sawed was pushed firmly against the upright projections ③. The side rest cleared the benchtop enough to prevent scarring of its surface.

SIDE CLAMPS

Long and lengthy boards could be conveniently edge-planed if they were raised and held vertically against the side of the workbench. A series of regularly spaced holes were bored into the bench apron. Wooden pegs were tapped in to support the work ~ the wider the board, the lower the row of pegs. The upper edge of the board was positioned a tad above the edge of the benchtop for unhindered planing.

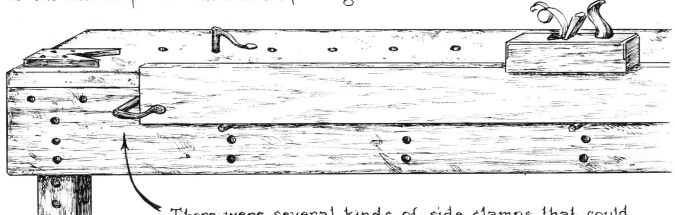

There were several kinds of side clamps that could be used to hold the work firmly against the bench apron:

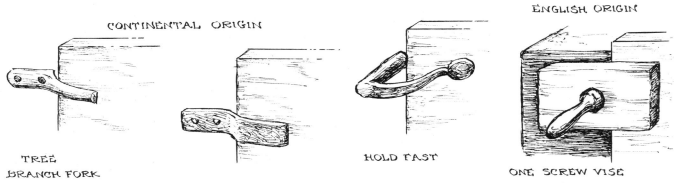

CONTINENTAL ORIGIN

ENGLISH ORIGIN

TREE
BRANCH FORK

HOLD FAST

ONE SCREW VISE

WROUGHT IRON ANGLE

HORIZONTAL AND VERTICAL BENCH VISES

The poorly defined tool on the left-hand corner of Moxon's workbench engraving was likely a single-handle screw vise.

It had two big brothers.

THE HORIZONTAL VERSION WAS MOUNTED LEVEL WITH THE BENCH-TOP. ITS CHUNKY OUTER JAW MOVED BY TURNING TWO SIZABLE WOODEN SCREWS EQUALLY, KEEPING IT PARALLEL TO THE FIXED INNER JAW. THE FRONT OF THE BENCH SERVED AS THE INNER JAW AND WAS BORED AND THREADED TO RECEIVE THE WOODEN SCREWS.

HORIZONTAL VISE

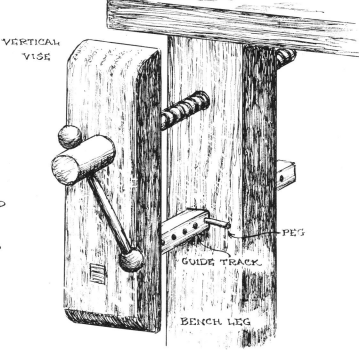

VERTICAL VISE

THE VERTICAL WOOD VISE WAS MOUNTED PERPENDICULAR TO AND LEVEL WITH THE BENCH TOP. A SINGLE LARGE WOODEN SCREW, ABOUT A FOOT BELOW THE BENCHTOP, MOVED THE HUSKY OUTER JAW. THE WORKTABLE LEG BECAME THE FIXED INNER JAW WITH ITS BORED AND THREADED SCREW HOLE.

SINCE THE TWO JAWS MUST BE KEPT PARALLEL TO EACH OTHER AS THEY SANDWICHED THE WORK, A SQUARED WOODEN GUIDE TRACK WAS MORTISED INTO THE LOWER END OF THE OUTER JAW. IT SLID FREELY INTO A SQUARED HOLE IN THE BENCH LEG. WHEN THE JAWS WERE TIGHTENED ON THE WORK, A PEG WAS MOUNTED INTO THE GUIDE-TRACK HOLE NEAREST THE BENCH LEG TO KEEP THE OUTER JAW PARALLEL TO THE INNER JAW.

PEG

GUIDE TRACK

BENCH LEG

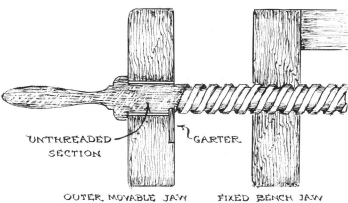

UNTHREADED SECTION

GARTER

OUTER MOVABLE JAW   FIXED BENCH JAW

THE SINGLE-HANDLE, THE HORIZONTAL, AND THE VERTICAL VISE ALL HAD AN INGENIOUS SCREWING MECHANISM IN COMMON. THE OUTER JAW WITH ITS UNTHREADED SECTION OF THE WOODEN SCREW WAS DRAWN CLOSED AS THE SCREW TURNED IN ITS THREADED WORK-BENCH HOLE, BUT THE OUTER JAW COULDN'T RETURN TO THE OPEN POSITION WITHOUT THE "GARTER." THIS HARDWOOD STRIP, MOR-TISED SECURELY INTO THE INNER FACE OF THE JAW, WAS PRESSED OUTWARD BY THE SCREW ACTION.

THE ROUNDER PLANE

The muscle behind the bench vise was the wooden screw. It called for a husky hardwood dowel of 2 or more inches in diameter. This was a job for the rounder plane.

THIS UNUSUAL PLANE HELD AN ORDINARY PLANE IRON, SLIGHTLY ROUNDED AT ITS CUTTING EDGES, AND COULD BE ADJUSTED FOR SHALLOW OR DEEP SHAVINGS. A STICK, ROUGHLY TRIMMED TO A CYLINDER WITH A DRAW KNIFE, WAS HELD AT ONE END IN A BENCH VISE. THE SLIGHTLY TAPERED CENTER HOLE OF THE ROUNDER PLANE WAS PUSHED ONTO THE FREE END OF THE STICK AND ROTATED. A SMOOTH WOODEN DOWEL WAS THE END RESULT.

ADJUSTMENT BOLT

PLANE IRON

SCREW BOX

THE DIAMETER OF THE DOWEL WAS THE SAME AS THE GUIDE HOLE ① IN THE FRONT PLATE. THE SHANK OF THE V CUTTER COULD BE ADJUSTED FOR DEEPER GROOVES OR REMOVED FOR SHARPENING BY LOOSENING THE HOOKED BOLT ②. THE CUTTER WAS POSITIONED AT THE START OF THIS THREADING WITH ONE END OF THE DOWEL LOCKED IN A BENCH VISE AND THE TWO SCREW-BOX PLATES JOINED WITH SCREWS ③. THE GUIDE HOLE ① WAS PUSHED OVER THE FREE END OF THE DOWEL. THE SPIRAL THREADS WERE CUT BY ROTATING THE HANDLES. THEY WERE KEPT REGULAR AND EQUAL BECAUSE THE NEW CUTS FOLLOWED THE SPIRAL THREADS IN THE SCREW BOX.

FRAMED TAP

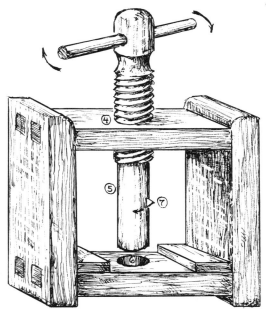

THE FRAMED TAP GROOVED FEMALE THREADS INTO A HOLE FOR ANY WOODEN SCREW THAT WAS OVER $\frac{3}{4}$-INCH IN DIAMETER. THE TOP PLATE OF THE FRAME HAD A THREADED HOLE ④ INTO WHICH WAS SCREWED A PARTIALLY THREADED WOODEN TAP CYLINDER. THE LOWER PORTION OF THE TAP ⑤ WAS UNTHREADED AND OF A LESSER DIAMETER, TO MATCH THE INNERMOST CUTS OF THE SCREW THREADS ④. ITS LOWER END FITTED INTO THE LOWER PLATE GUIDE HOLE ⑥.

IN PRACTICE, THE SAW BLOCK TO BE THREADED WAS DRILLED WITH A BIT AND BRACE OF THE SAME DIAMETER AS THE UNTHREADED TAP SECTION ⑤.

INNER DIAMETER

94

WITH THE LOWER PLATE SECURED IN A BENCH VISE AND THE WORK POSITIONED OVER THE GUIDE HOLE ⑥, THE TAP HANDLES WERE ROTATED. THE V-SHAPED CUTTING BLADE ⑦ SLICED OUT THE THREADS AS THE TAP TWISTED DOWN THROUGH THE BORED HOLE IN THE WORK. WHEN FINISHED THE WOODEN SCREW SHOULD TURN FREELY INTO THE NEWLY THREADED JAW OF THE VISE.

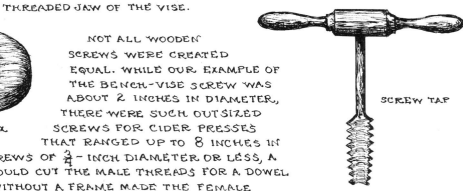

NOT ALL WOODEN SCREWS WERE CREATED EQUAL. WHILE OUR EXAMPLE OF THE BENCH-VISE SCREW WAS ABOUT 2 INCHES IN DIAMETER, THERE WERE SUCH OUTSIZED SCREWS FOR CIDER PRESSES THAT RANGED UP TO 8 INCHES IN DIAMETER. FOR WOODEN SCREWS OF $\frac{3}{4}$-INCH DIAMETER OR LESS, A SINGLE BLOCK SCREW BOX WOULD CUT THE MALE THREADS FOR A DOWEL AND THE STEEL SCREW TAP WITHOUT A FRAME MADE THE FEMALE THREADS FOR THE SCREW HOLE.

SINGLE BLOCK MALE SCREW BOX

SCREW TAP

WOODTURNING TOOLS

POLE LATHE

When it came to the lathe, woodworking tools took a different twist. By rotating a stick rapidly between two greased iron pins or "pikes," graceful shapes could be shaved out with a variety of woodturning tools.

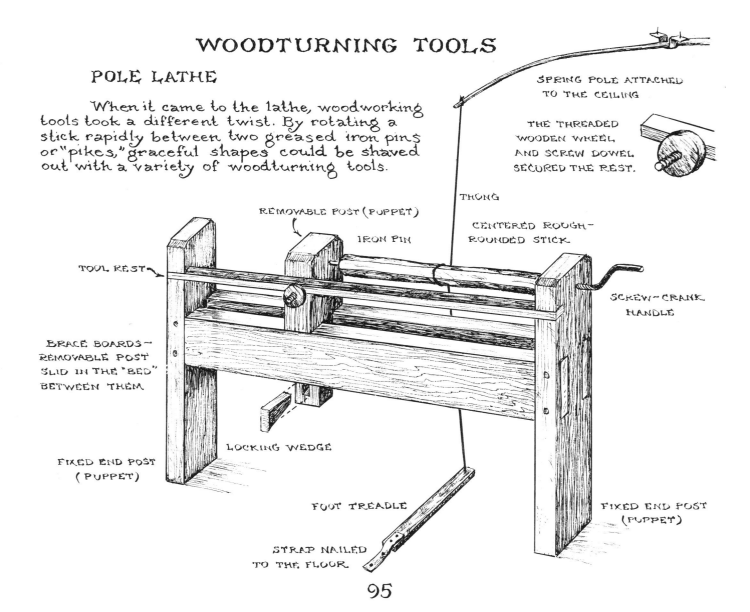

SPRING POLE ATTACHED TO THE CEILING

THE THREADED WOODEN WHEEL AND SCREW DOWEL SECURED THE REST.

THONG

CENTERED ROUGH-ROUNDED STICK

REMOVABLE POST (PUPPET)

IRON PIN

TOOL REST

SCREW-CRANK HANDLE

BRACE BOARDS~ REMOVABLE POST SLID IN THE "BED" BETWEEN THEM

LOCKING WEDGE

FIXED END POST (PUPPET)

FIXED END POST (PUPPET)

FOOT TREADLE

STRAP NAILED TO THE FLOOR

The curvaceous balusters in the Georgian staircases were one of many useful turnings that came from the lathe. Yet this simple tool was usually made by the woodcrafter without much effort. Its design really hadn't changed since the ancients discovered its usefulness. But new sources of power have so improved the efficiency and performance of the lathe that the tool remains one of the most valued in today's workshop.

FROM
JOHANN AMOS COMENIUS,
ORBIS SENSUALIUM PICTUS,
1685

The pole lathe had its problems. Only when the foot treadle was depressed could the turning chisel shave into the revolving wood. Releasing the treadle caused the spring pole to pull upward on the thong, reversing the direction of the rotation. Then the chisel must be pulled away from the work. Further, the thong must be looped around the center of the work to spin it properly. Obviously the turning chisels must avoid that section. There was a better way.

THE GREAT WHEEL LATHE

A lathe that turned in but one direction? This long-term dream came true in the early eighteenth century when a 6-foot wheel could do just that. Professional cabinet shops were quick to join this "revolution" in woodturning.

CRANK

SPINDLE

REVOLVING PIPE

TOOL REST

REMOVABLE POST WEDGE

An apprentice turned the great wheel (a less than inspiring chore) with its crank, giving a forceful and continuous rotation to the lathe spindle. The two revolving iron points were centered and tightened firmly into the work.

TURNING TOOLS

TANG

TAPERED ⟶ BULBOUS   FERRULE

Unlike the common carpenters' chisels, turning chisels had longer blades, with plain tapered tangs. Handles were also lengthy in colonial times, bulbous near the ferrule and tapered toward the opposite end.

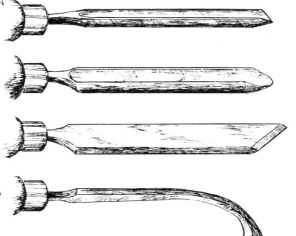

THE V-TOOL SCORED THE DESIGN SPACINGS ON THE REVOLVING WORK. THE CUTTING EDGE WAS V-SHAPED WITH AN OUTER BEVEL.

GOUGES REMOVED UNWANTED WOOD IN A HURRY AS WELL AS CUTTING ROUNDED GROOVES. THEY WERE CONCAVE WITH OUTER BEVELS.

CHISELS SMOOTHED THE SURFACE OF THE WORK WITH SQUARE OR ANGLED CUTTING EDGES WITH INNER AND OUTER BEVELS.

HOOK AND SIDE TOOLS HOLLOWED AND UNDERCUT BOWLS WITH ITS OUTER BEVEL-HOOKED BLADE. GENERALLY THE WORK WAS SECURED TO THE REVOLVING PIKE WITH A FACE PLATE.

THE PARTING CHISEL FREED THE END OF THE FINISHED TURNING BY UNDERCUTTING THE ENDS OF THE WORK. THE BLADE FACES WERE BEVEL-TAPERED TO GIVE A CUTTING EDGE THAT WAS THE DEPTH OF THE BLADE.

The top edge of the tool rest was slightly below the axis of the work. For close-grained hardwoods, the cutting edge of the turning tool was raised slightly above the axis. Soft woods required more of a raised angle of the tool to prevent gouging and splintering.

TOOL REST

TURNING HARDWOOD   TURNING SOFTWOOD   TOOL REST

CALIPERS

These wooden or iron tools had two or more movable legs for measuring the outer and inner diameters of lathe work. The outer measurement between two points on a model or pattern could be transferred and compared with the spinning work on the lathe. It would be a sorry table, chair, or bed that had legs of different size and shape turnings. Inner measurements would be used to check the inside diameter of a turned bowl or box.

OUTSIDE DIAMETER

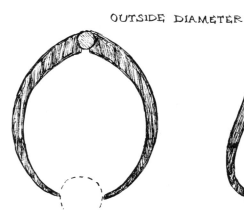

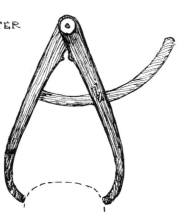

OUTSIDE DIAMETER

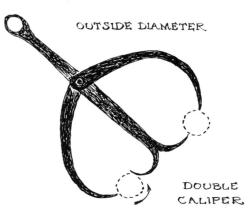

BOW CALIPER
WOODEN BOWED LEGS
(MERCER, ANCIENT CARPENTERS' TOOLS, 1960, PAGE 228)

WING CALIPER
WOODEN WING AND LEGS

DOUBLE CALIPER
AN IRON TOOL WITH A LEFT LEG CURVED UP TO PREVENT POINT FROM DIGGING INTO THE SPINNING WORK.
(SHELBURNE MUSEUM, SHELBURNE, VERMONT)

INSIDE/OUTSIDE DIAMETERS

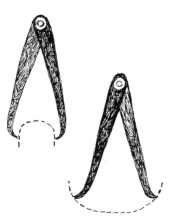

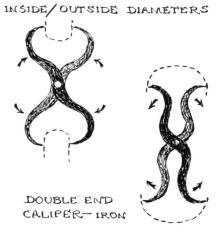

STRAIGHT CALIPER ~ IRON
CROSSING THE IRON LEGS GAVE INSIDE OR OUTSIDE DIAMETER.

DOUBLE END CALIPER ~ IRON
PATTERN AND WORK COULD BE COMPARED WITH EITHER INSIDE OR OUTSIDE DIAMETERS.

INSIDE AND OUTSIDE CALIPER ~ IRON

Many of the calipers were handmade. The pivot joints were tight and stiff enough to hold the jaw setting, although some did have a locking thumb screw or the like.

ALL ABOUT PUMP LOGS

There was one last step before the colonial post-and-beam house could be called a home. Some sort of water supply was needed— a spring, well, or perhaps a town reservoir. Wooden pipes, better known as pump logs because they had long carried well water drawn up by hand pumps, were from freshly cut logs from almost any stand of straight trees.

The green logs, ranging from 8 to 16 feet, were center-bored with the twisted cylinder auger or the pod auger. There would be no shrinking and checking with the unseasoned wood. One end of each log was shaved to an outer tapered male cone, and the opposite end was reamed out as an inner female receiver. Then each joint was smeared with tallow for a snug watertight fit. The wooden pipes were placed in a dug trench. The male and female joints were driven together with a large mallet. When covered with dirt and the water flowing, the joints became swollen and leakproof. Pump logs have been found that are three centuries old— and still very workable.

TWISTED CYLINDER AUGER

AS THE CARPENTER KEPT A
STEADY FORWARD PRESSURE, THE LENGTHY HALF CYLINDER
WITH ONE SHARPENED EDGE KEPT THE BORING ON A STRAIGHT COURSE DOWN THE
CENTER OF THE LOG. BECAUSE OF THE CONSIDERABLE FRICTION CAUSED BY ITS
LENGTH, TWO MEN WERE OFTEN NEEDED TO MOVE THE AUGER AHEAD. FORTUNATELY
THE BIT TAPERED INTO A SPIRAL CUTTER THAT ENDED IN A SMALL SCREW. THE
HALF CYLINDER WAS DRAWN THROUGH THE CENTER OF THE LOG. THE AUGER'S
SHAPE HELD THE SHAVINGS AND HAD TO BE WITHDRAWN FREQUENTLY TO
PREVENT CLOGGING.

POD AUGER

THE SHORT AND ROUNDED
SIDES DID INDEED RESEMBLE A SEED POD.
THE SHARPENED EDGE TWISTED INTO A POINT TO CUT AND DRAW THE BORING
FORWARD. ALTHOUGH THE SHAPE GAVE CONSIDERABLY LESS FRICTION THAN
THE TWISTED CYLINDER AUGER, IT WAS LESS ACCURATE IN ITS COURSE. THE
POD AUGER ALSO HELD THE SHAVINGS THAT MUST BE EMPTIED REGULARLY.

THE POD AUGER ALSO HELD THE SHAVINGS THAT MUST BE EMPTIED REGULARLY.

SPOUT CUTTER

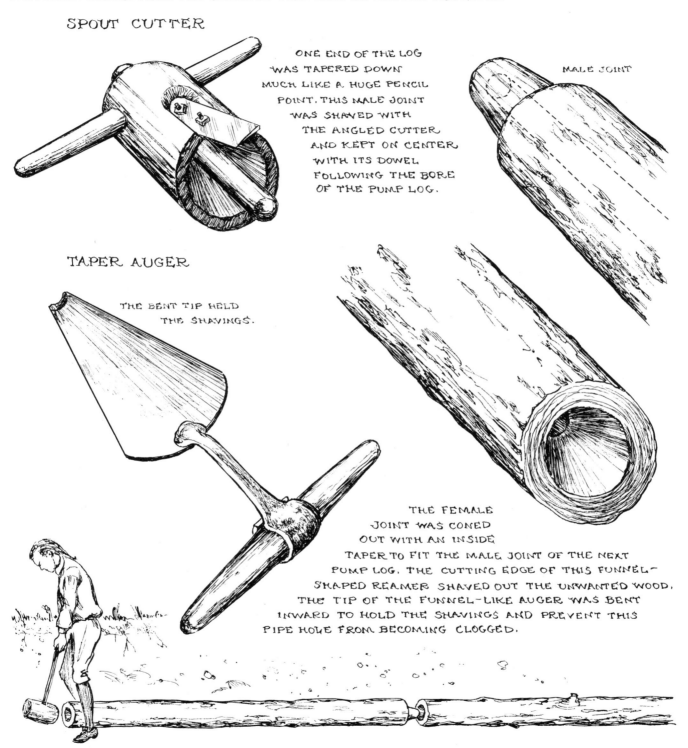

ONE END OF THE LOG WAS TAPERED DOWN MUCH LIKE A HUGE PENCIL POINT. THIS MALE JOINT WAS SHAVED WITH THE ANGLED CUTTER AND KEPT ON CENTER WITH ITS DOWEL FOLLOWING THE BORE OF THE PUMP LOG.

MALE JOINT

TAPER AUGER

THE BENT TIP HELD THE SHAVINGS.

THE FEMALE JOINT WAS CONED OUT WITH AN INSIDE TAPER TO FIT THE MALE JOINT OF THE NEXT PUMP LOG. THE CUTTING EDGE OF THIS FUNNEL-SHAPED REAMER SHAVED OUT THE UNWANTED WOOD. THE TIP OF THE FUNNEL-LIKE AUGER WAS BENT INWARD TO HOLD THE SHAVINGS AND PREVENT THIS PIPE HOLE FROM BECOMING CLOGGED.

100

ADVANCES IN WOODWORKING TOOLS

FOR A COMPARISON OF TOOLS USED ON
OUR NOW COMPLETED AMERICAN COLONIAL
HOME AND THEIR PREDECESSORS OF OTHER
CENTURIES, THE FOLLOWING PAGES MAY BE
HELPFUL. THE BRIEF OUTLINE ALSO HIGH~
LIGHTS THE CHANGES THAT MAKE OUR
MODERN HANDTOOLS SO USEFUL.

ADZ

The blade was set at right angles to the handle for smoothing, shaping, or trimming timber. Most had wedge-shaped eyes that tightened against the handle with every swing. To sharpen the inner bevel cutting edge, the length of the handle was driven out through the eye.

CHANNELED
GOUGE

STONE

5000~3000 B.C.
EARLY ARCHAIC INDIANS
GOUGED OUT CHAR FROM
DUGOUT CANOES AND BOWLS.

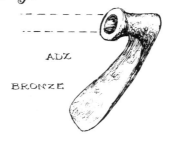

ADZ

BRONZE

2700 B.C.
BABYLONIA
EARLY EYE FOR HANDLE

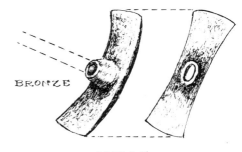

BRONZE

2000 B.C.
CRETE
DOUBLE BLADE WITH EYE HOLE

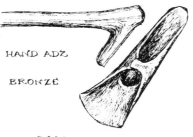

HAND ADZ

BRONZE

2000~1500 B.C.
MIDDLE EAST AND EUROPE
CAST LOOPS

HAND ADZ

COPPER
LATER BRONZE

1650~1450 B.C.
EGYPT
LASHED BLADE CROOK HANDLE

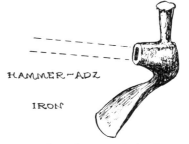

HAMMER-ADZ

IRON

900 B.C.~A.D. 400
ROME
ELLIPTICAL EYE

HAND ADZ

STONE

300~1675
CERAMIC-WOODLAND
INDIANS

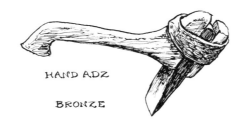

HAND ADZ

BRONZE

150~400
EGYPT
IRON COLLAR AND WEDGE

IRON

950~1000
SCANDINAVIA
FLARED CUTTING EDGE

HAND
HAMMER-ADZ

STEEL

1700~1800
FRANCE-DIDEROT

HAND
GOUGE-ADZ

STEEL

1700~1800
FRANCE-DIDEROT

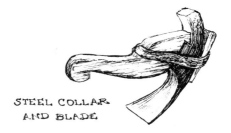

STEEL COLLAR
AND BLADE

1700~1800
FRANCE-DIDEROT

103

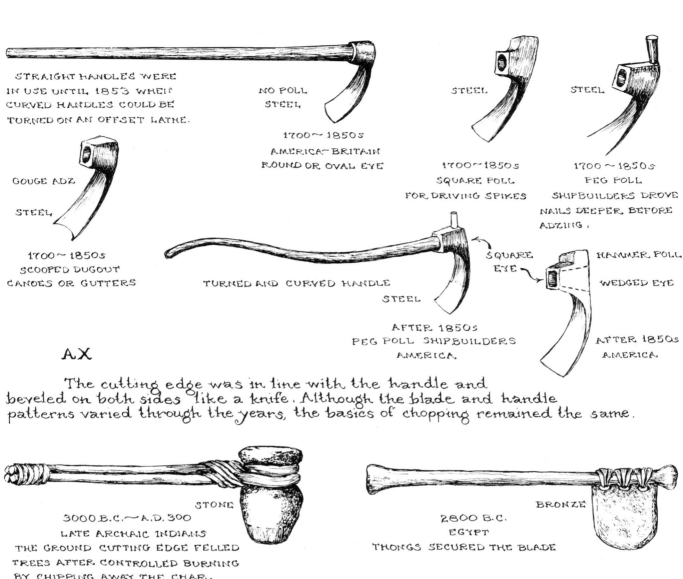

STRAIGHT HANDLES WERE IN USE UNTIL 1853 WHEN CURVED HANDLES COULD BE TURNED ON AN OFFSET LATHE.

NO POLL STEEL

1700~1850s AMERICA~BRITAIN ROUND OR OVAL EYE

STEEL

1700~1850s SQUARE POLL FOR DRIVING SPIKES

STEEL

1700~1850s PEG POLL SHIPBUILDERS DROVE NAILS DEEPER BEFORE ADZING.

GOUGE ADZ STEEL

1700~1850s SCOOPED DUGOUT CANOES OR GUTTERS

TURNED AND CURVED HANDLE STEEL

AFTER 1850s PEG POLL SHIPBUILDERS AMERICA

SQUARE EYE

HAMMER POLL WEDGED EYE

AFTER 1850s AMERICA

AX

The cutting edge was in line with the handle and beveled on both sides like a knife. Although the blade and handle patterns varied through the years, the basics of chopping remained the same.

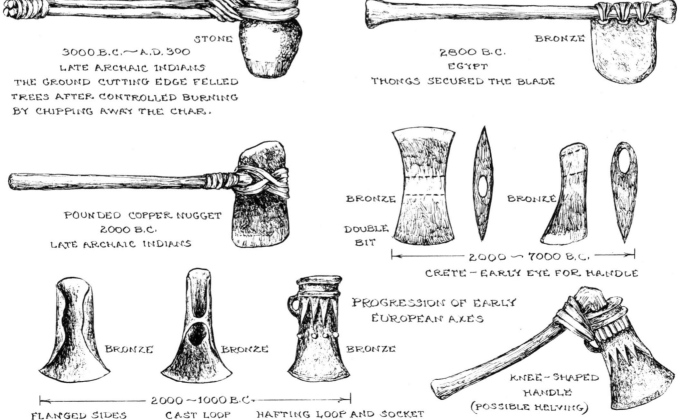

STONE
3000 B.C.~A.D. 300
LATE ARCHAIC INDIANS
THE GROUND CUTTING EDGE FELLED TREES AFTER CONTROLLED BURNING BY CHIPPING AWAY THE CHAR.

BRONZE
2800 B.C.
EGYPT
THONGS SECURED THE BLADE

POUNDED COPPER NUGGET
2000 B.C.
LATE ARCHAIC INDIANS

BRONZE
DOUBLE BIT

BRONZE

2000~7000 B.C.
CRETE~EARLY EYE FOR HANDLE

PROGRESSION OF EARLY EUROPEAN AXES

BRONZE

BRONZE

BRONZE

2000~1000 B.C.
FLANGED SIDES   CAST LOOP   HAFTING LOOP AND SOCKET

KNEE-SHAPED HANDLE (POSSIBLE HELVING)

SOME ROMAN AXES WERE PARTLY STEEL.

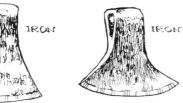

IRON FELLING · IRON FELLING · IRON FELLING · DOUBLE BIT · IRON AX-ADZ · IRON AX-HAMMER

|← 900 B.C. ~ A.D. 400 →|

ALL ROMAN—THE FIRST TO BEND A HOT STRIP OF IRON AT THE CENTER TO FORM
AN EYE AND FLAT POLL. THESE WERE THE TRADITIONAL FORMS FOR THE LATER
CENTURIES. ALL WERE HAFTED WITH STRAIGHT WOODEN HANDLES.

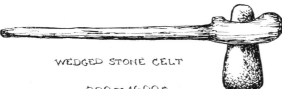

WEDGED STONE CELT

300 ~ 1600s
CERAMIC - WOODLAND INDIANS
REMOVED CHAR FROM BURNING

IRON · IRON · IRON

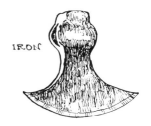

500 ~ 1500 MEDIEVAL EUROPE
REINFORCED EYES FOR HANDLES

IRON

500 ~ 1500
MEDIEVAL EUROPE
T- AX WITH ROUND POLL

ENLARGING THE POLL
NONE › · SMALL › · ENLARGED › LUG · LARGE POLL › LUG

UNBALANCED BIT · BALANCED BIT

1600 ~ 1740
COLONIAL TRADE AX

1740
ANGLO-AMERICAN

1750
AMERICA

AN ELONGATED BIT (BLADE) WOBBLED WHEN SWUNG. SHORTENING IT WHILE ENLARGING
THE POLL GAVE THE BALANCED AND SMOOTH-CHOPPING AMERICAN AX. NOTE THE LUGS
THAT GAVE MORE CONTACT WITH
THE HANDLE.

UNTIL 1853, ALL AX HANDLES WERE STRAIGHT.
THAT YEAR CURVED AX HANDLES WERE BEING TURNED
ON A NEW KIND OF LATHE FOR TURNING GUNSTOCKS.

1840 TO THE PRESENT
THE DOUBLE - BITTED AX

IS STILL USED BY AMERICAN LUMBERMEN
AND STILL HAS THE OLD STRAIGHT HANDLE FOR
FELLING WITH EITHER BIT. WHEN ONE BIT DULLED,
THE AXMAN USED THE OTHER WITHOUT RESHARPENING
DURING THE DAY'S WORK.

1850 TO THE PRESENT
ENGLISH

AUGER

This T-shaped drill specialized in the boring of large holes in thick boards ~ but only after a good deal of heavy clockwise handle-twisting and body pressure to make it behave.

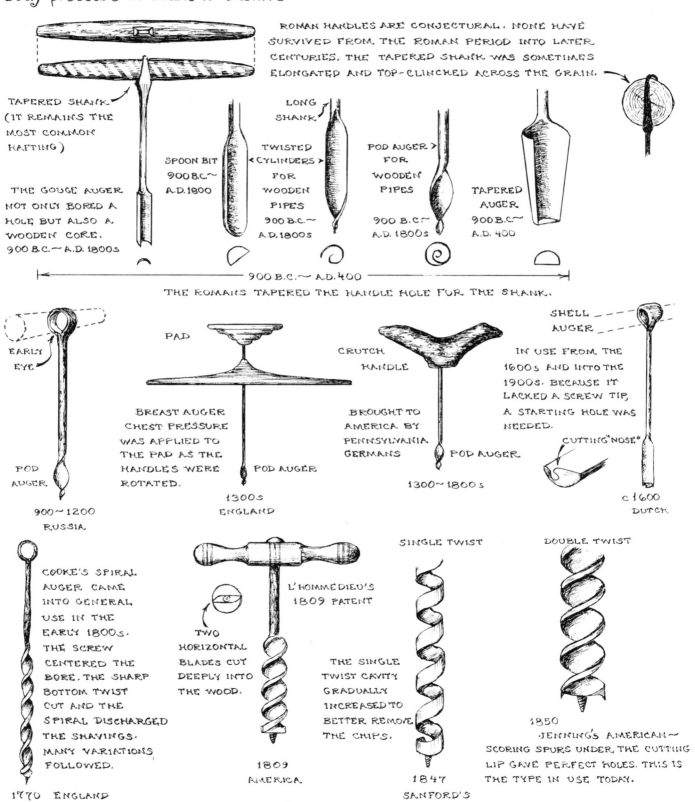

ROMAN HANDLES ARE CONJECTURAL. NONE HAVE SURVIVED FROM THE ROMAN PERIOD INTO LATER CENTURIES. THE TAPERED SHANK WAS SOMETIMES ELONGATED AND TOP-CLINCHED ACROSS THE GRAIN.

TAPERED SHANK (IT REMAINS THE MOST COMMON HAFTING)

THE GOUGE AUGER NOT ONLY BORED A HOLE BUT ALSO A WOODEN CORE. 900 B.C. ~ A.D. 1800s

SPOON BIT 900 B.C. ~ A.D. 1800

TWISTED CYLINDERS FOR WOODEN PIPES 900 B.C. ~ A.D. 1800s

POD AUGER FOR WOODEN PIPES 900 B.C. ~ A.D. 1800s

TAPERED AUGER 900 B.C. ~ A.D. 400

900 B.C. ~ A.D. 400

THE ROMANS TAPERED THE HANDLE HOLE FOR THE SHANK.

EARLY EYE

PAD

CRUTCH HANDLE

SHELL AUGER

BREAST AUGER CHEST PRESSURE WAS APPLIED TO THE PAD AS THE HANDLES WERE ROTATED.

POD AUGER

BROUGHT TO AMERICA BY PENNSYLVANIA GERMANS

POD AUGER

IN USE FROM THE 1600s AND INTO THE 1900s. BECAUSE IT LACKED A SCREW TIP, A STARTING HOLE WAS NEEDED.

CUTTING "NOSE"

POD AUGER 900 ~ 1200 RUSSIA.

1300s ENGLAND

1300 ~ 1800s

c 1600 DUTCH

COOKE'S SPIRAL AUGER CAME INTO GENERAL USE IN THE EARLY 1800s. THE SCREW CENTERED THE BORE. THE SHARP BOTTOM TWIST CUT AND THE SPIRAL DISCHARGED THE SHAVINGS. MANY VARIATIONS FOLLOWED.

1770 ENGLAND

TWO HORIZONTAL BLADES CUT DEEPLY INTO THE WOOD.

L'HOMMEDIEU'S 1809 PATENT

1809 AMERICA

THE SINGLE TWIST CAVITY GRADUALLY INCREASED TO BETTER REMOVE THE CHIPS.

SINGLE TWIST

1847 SANFORD'S INCREMENTAL TWIST

DOUBLE TWIST

1850 JENNING'S AMERICAN ~ SCORING SPURS UNDER THE CUTTING LIP GAVE PERFECT HOLES. THIS IS THE TYPE IN USE TODAY.

BRACE AND BIT

The brace and bit were relatively new kids on the wood block. Not until the 1400s did the combination first appear in Europe ~ and then only start pilot holes for augers. Its usefulness for boring small holes was soon appreciated. Through the later centuries, most improvements had to do with securing and interchanging bits in the brace chuck.

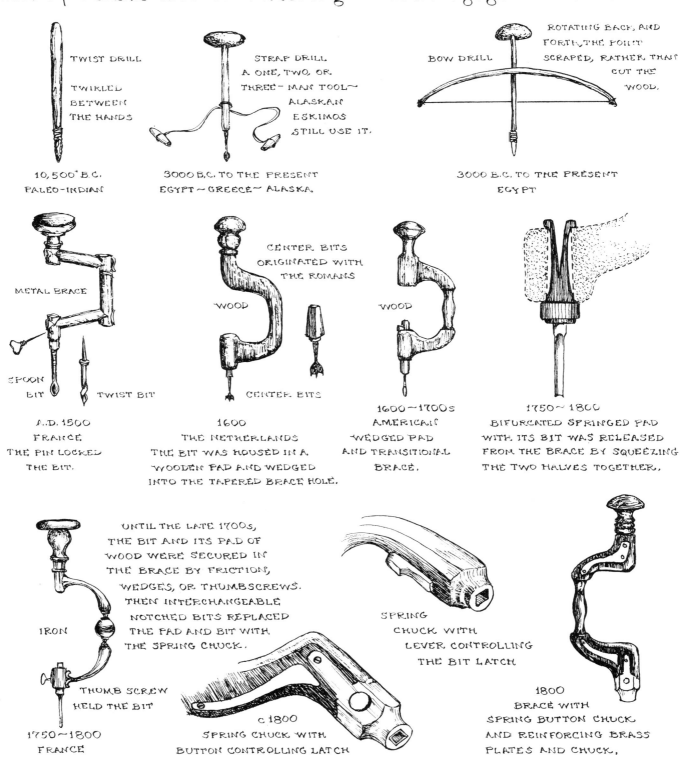

TWIST DRILL

TWIRLED BETWEEN THE HANDS

10,500+ B.C.
PALEO-INDIAN

STRAP DRILL
A ONE, TWO, OR THREE ~ MAN TOOL ~ ALASKAN ESKIMOS STILL USE IT.

3000 B.C. TO THE PRESENT
EGYPT ~ GREECE ~ ALASKA

BOW DRILL

ROTATING BACK AND FORTH, THE POINT SCRAPED, RATHER THAN CUT THE WOOD.

3000 B.C. TO THE PRESENT
EGYPT

METAL BRACE

SPOON BIT   TWIST BIT

A.D. 1500
FRANCE
THE PIN LOCKED THE BIT.

CENTER BITS ORIGINATED WITH THE ROMANS

WOOD

CENTER BITS

1600
THE NETHERLANDS
THE BIT WAS HOUSED IN A WOODEN PAD AND WEDGED INTO THE TAPERED BRACE HOLE.

WOOD

1600 ~ 1700s
AMERICAN WEDGED PAD AND TRANSITIONAL BRACE.

1750 ~ 1800
BIFURCATED SPRINGED PAD WITH ITS BIT WAS RELEASED FROM THE BRACE BY SQUEEZING THE TWO HALVES TOGETHER.

IRON

THUMB SCREW HELD THE BIT

1750 ~ 1800
FRANCE

UNTIL THE LATE 1700s, THE BIT AND ITS PAD OF WOOD WERE SECURED IN THE BRACE BY FRICTION, WEDGES, OR THUMBSCREWS. THEN INTERCHANGEABLE NOTCHED BITS REPLACED THE PAD AND BIT WITH THE SPRING CHUCK.

c 1800
SPRING CHUCK WITH BUTTON CONTROLLING LATCH

SPRING CHUCK WITH LEVER CONTROLLING THE BIT LATCH

1800
BRACE WITH SPRING BUTTON CHUCK AND REINFORCING BRASS PLATES AND CHUCK.

107

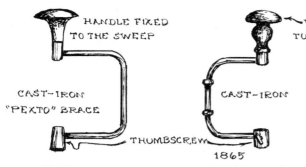

HANDLE FIXED
TO THE SWEEP

CAST-IRON
"PEXTO" BRACE

THUMBSCREW

1850
THIS FIRST AMERICAN
FACTORY-MADE BRACE
HELD ITS BIT IN
THE SQUARE SOCKET
WITH A THUMBSCREW.

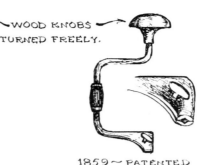

WOOD KNOBS
TURNED FREELY.

CAST-IRON

THUMBSCREW

1865
IMPROVED MODEL WAS
LIGHTER BUT HAD A
THUMBSCREW AND
SOCKET THAT FITTED
ONLY THE MAKER'S BITS.

1859 ~ PATENTED
1866 ~ POPULARIZED
THE AMERICAN SPOFFORD
BRACE COULD HOLD ANY
SQUARE-SHANKED BIT.

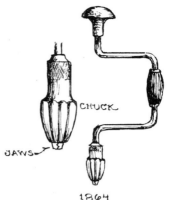

CHUCK

JAWS

1864
THE BARBER BRACE
USED A SCREWED SHELL
CHUCK TO OPEN THE
JAWS FOR ANY BIT. A
RACHET WAS ADDED IN 1865.

BROADAX

This hewer of timber had its cutting edge beveled only on the right side. The eye also bulged to the right to give a perfectly flat face to the left side of the blade next to the log being squared. The short handle bent to the right as well, to prevent bashed knuckles. Hewing hatchets were generally smaller versions of their big brothers, the broadaxes.

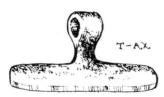

T-AX

A.D. 700 ~ 1300
BRITAIN AND EUROPEAN

MEDIEVAL MANUSCRIPTS FREQUENTLY SHOWED THE T-AX BEING USED AS A SIDE AX FOR SQUARING OR TRIMMING THE EDGES OF TIMBER. PERHAPS THROUGH THE CENTURIES THAT FOLLOWED, THE EYE WAS FLATTENED TO SLICE CLOSE TO THE WOOD. PERHAPS THE CUTTING EDGE WAS CHANGED FROM THE V-KNIFE EDGE OF THE AX TO THE V-CHISEL EDGE OF THE BROADAX. ENGLAND AND THE CONTINENT DEVELOPED THE DIFFERENT STYLES THAT WERE BROUGHT TO THE COLONIES.

BRITAIN-AMERICA

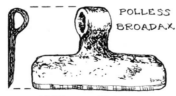

POLLESS
BROADAX

1600s ~ 1800s
SQUARE BLADES WERE
FAVORED BY COOPERS
AND SHIPBUILDERS.

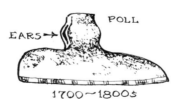

EARS →

POLL

1700 ~ 1800s
AS WITH AXES, THE POLL
HELPED TO BALANCE THE
WEIGHT OF THE BLADE.

1750 ~ 1800s
A HEAVIER POLL
IMPROVED HEWING.

1750-1800s
DOUBLE EARS AND
A HEAVY POLL.

1750 ~ 1800s

1850 ~ 1900
STYLE UNCHANGED

108

GERMAN-AMERICAN GOOSEWING POLLESS BROADAX

A.D. 1500s~1700s
GERMANY

1600s~1700s
PENNSYLVANIA

THE GOOSEWING BROADAX WAS BROUGHT TO AMERICA BY PENNSYLVANIA GERMANS.

1700s~1800s
PENNSYLVANIA

1700s~1800s
PENNSYLVANIA

c. 1800s
PENNSYLVANIA

CHISELS

The earliest chisels were chipped or forged with the blade and handle in one piece. Later chisels were forged with either a socket or a tang for securing the handle. Most had cutting edges with a single bevel.

Forming chisels with flat sturdy blades were used with a mallet for general woodworking. Paring chisels had lighter blades that were pushed and not struck with a mallet. They smoothed and refined the work. Flat-bladed mortise chisels were heavy-duty tools for use with a mallet. Gouge blades were curved on cross section for hollowing or scooping away unwanted wood. Special purpose chisels of varied blade shapes and sizes were used by woodcarvers, woodturners, and others.

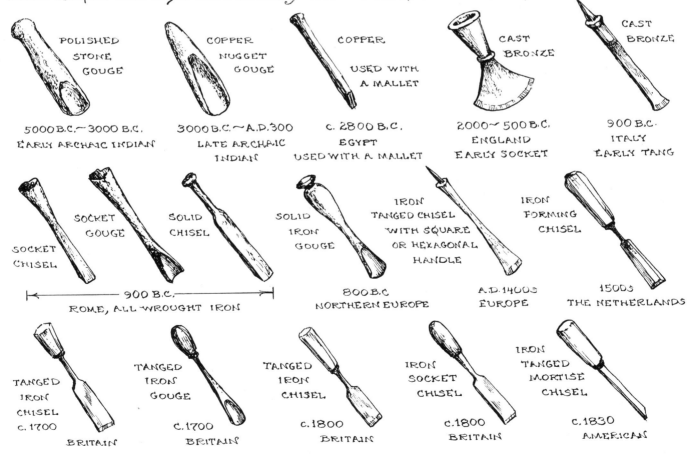

POLISHED STONE GOUGE
5000 B.C.~3000 B.C.
EARLY ARCHAIC INDIAN

COPPER NUGGET GOUGE
3000 B.C.~A.D.300
LATE ARCHAIC INDIAN

COPPER USED WITH A MALLET
c. 2800 B.C.
EGYPT
USED WITH A MALLET

CAST BRONZE
2000~500 B.C.
ENGLAND
EARLY SOCKET

CAST BRONZE
900 B.C.
ITALY
EARLY TANG

SOCKET CHISEL
SOCKET GOUGE
SOLID CHISEL
900 B.C.
ROME, ALL WROUGHT IRON

SOLID IRON GOUGE
IRON TANGED CHISEL WITH SQUARE OR HEXAGONAL HANDLE
800 B.C.
NORTHERN EUROPE

IRON FORMING CHISEL
A.D. 1400s
EUROPE

1500s
THE NETHERLANDS

TANGED IRON CHISEL
c. 1700
BRITAIN

TANGED IRON GOUGE
c. 1700
BRITAIN

TANGED IRON CHISEL
c. 1800
BRITAIN

IRON SOCKET CHISEL
c. 1800
BRITAIN

IRON TANGED MORTISE CHISEL
c. 1830
AMERICAN

HAMMERS

When prehistoric man realized that a fist-sized stone was a handy tool for cracking nuts, shellfish, and marrow bones for food, he'd discovered the hammer. Paleo-Indians used the hammerstone to chip stone knives, scrapers, fluted spear points, and drill points. Then this earliest of tools underwent "striking" changes when metals could be cast or wrought. The claw hammer was the brainchild of the Romans. Looking much like the hammers of today, it had a face for pounding, an eye to hold the handle, and a claw for pulling nails. But when the light handle in it's small eye was used as a lever for removing wayward~ and valuable~ nails, the breakage must have been considerable.

By the 1400s, reinforcing iron straps were stop-gap solutions for handle breakage. A pair of straps could be riveted to both sides of the handle, passed through the eye, and then bent over the hammer head. Or the head could be wrought with straps for securing to the handle. Either way, replacing a damaged handle must have been a chore and a half. Not until 1840 did an American blacksmith invent a long adz-eye that kept the head where it belonged~ on a sturdy handle. We've appreciated his inventiveness ever since in our workshops.

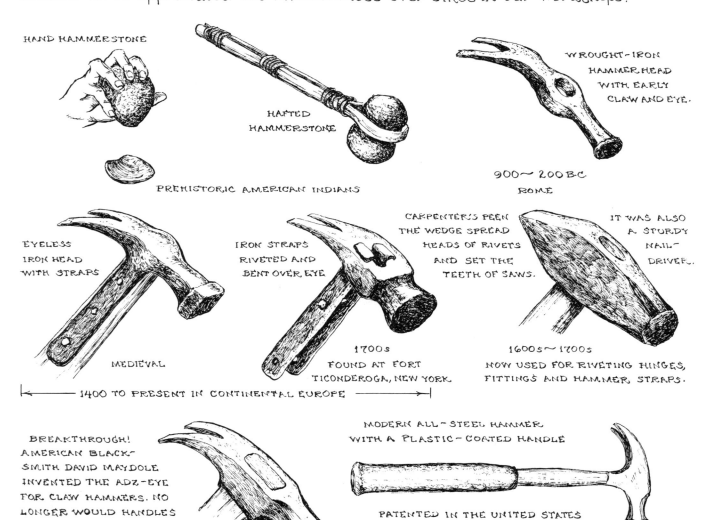

HAND HAMMERSTONE

HAFTED HAMMERSTONE

PREHISTORIC AMERICAN INDIANS

WROUGHT-IRON HAMMER HEAD WITH EARLY CLAW AND EYE.

900~200 B.C.
ROME

EYELESS IRON HEAD WITH STRAPS

MEDIEVAL

IRON STRAPS RIVETED AND BENT OVER EYE

1700s
FOUND AT FORT TICONDEROGA, NEW YORK

CARPENTER'S PEEN THE WEDGE SPREAD HEADS OF RIVETS AND SET THE TEETH OF SAWS.

IT WAS ALSO A STURDY NAIL-DRIVER.

1600s~1700s
NOW USED FOR RIVETING HINGES, FITTINGS AND HAMMER STRAPS.

|←——— 1400 TO PRESENT IN CONTINENTAL EUROPE ———→|

BREAKTHROUGH! AMERICAN BLACK-SMITH DAVID MAYDOLE INVENTED THE ADZ-EYE FOR CLAW HAMMERS. NO LONGER WOULD HANDLES BE WRENCHED INTO SPLINTERS WHEN NAILS WERE PULLED.

1840

MODERN ALL-STEEL HAMMER WITH A PLASTIC-COATED HANDLE

PATENTED IN THE UNITED STATES BY ERNEST ESTWING IN 1926.

PLANES

When it came to the shaping, smoothing, and straight-edging of wood, the Egyptians had a problem. At hand were only chisels, saws, and adzes for the job, and perhaps sandstone for the final smoothing. Then the Romans discovered that wood could be shaved at a controlled depth by wedging a chisel blade aslant in a block with an iron sole. The basic bench plane had joined the woodworking tool family.

The Romans designed the bench plane for specific uses. The jack plane held a slightly convex cutting blade for shaving off amounts of excess wood. The small smoothing plane's straight cutting edge smoothed out the rough scoop cuts made by the jack plane. Probably the Romans also developed the trying plane. Also known as the truing or jointer plane, its considerable length planed a level track for "truing" up straight edges for boards to be joined together.

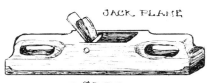

JACK PLANE

c. 50 B.C.
ROME
TOTE HANDLES FOR CARRYING

SMOOTHING PLANE

c. 50 B.C.
ROME
CROSSBAR HELD THE WEDGE.

1514 (FROM DÜRER)
NORTHERN EUROPEANS HAD A FRONT HAND KNOB AND EARLY SIDE GROOVES FOR WEDGE.

TRYING PLANE

1600s ~ EARLY 1700s
ENGLAND AND CONTINENTAL EUROPE
FOR THESE LONGER PLANES, A CROOK HANDLE TOTE FOR CARRYING WAS ADDED TO THE FRONT KNOB OR "HORN." MANY LARGE JACK PLANES WERE ALSO PROVIDED WITH THESE FRONT AND REAR HANDLES.

TRYING PLANE

1735 ~ 1750
ENGLAND AND AMERICA
A NEW AND STURDIER TOTE GAVE THE CRAFTSMAN A SOLID GRIP ON THE PLANE ~ SO MUCH SO THAT THE ENGLISH DROPPED THE FRONT HAND GRIP.

SMOOTHING PLANE

1600s ~ 1700s
NORTHERN EUROPE
SQUARE STOCK WITH AN UPRIGHT HAND GRIP

1650 ~ 1700s
ENGLISH AND AMERICAN
CURVED SIDES PERMITTED A WIDER CUTTING IRON. IT SURVIVES AS THE ENGLISH "COFFIN" PLANE.

DOUBLE IRON ~ THE EARLIEST CAP IRONS WERE WEDGED IN PLACE.

c. 1780s
THE CAP CURLED THE SHAVINGS AND COULD PLANE AGAINST GRAIN.

JACK AND TRYING PLANES

1828 ~ 1880
UNITED STATES
FACTORY ~ MADE

JACK PLANE

1827
KNOWLES'S PATENT IRON PLANE. THE FIRST IRON PLANE SINCE THE ROMANS. THIS AMERICAN PLANE WAS WEDGED IN CAST SIDE RIBS.

TRYING PLANE

1858 AMERICAN ~ BAILEY'S FIRST PATENT VERTICAL BLADE ADJUSTMENT AND A CAMMED LEVER CAP.

111

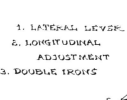

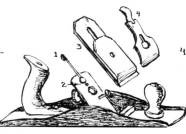

1. LATERAL LEVER
2. LONGITUDINAL ADJUSTMENT
3. DOUBLE IRONS

4. CAMMED LEVER ON IRON CAP
5. CAST IRON

1867
BAILEY BENCH PLANE
A BOAT-SHAPED CASTING WAS BEDDED IN A WOODEN STOCK. A LEVER AND KNOB ADJUSTED THE THIN CUTTING IRON.

THE MODERN BENCH PLANE
THIS USER-FRIENDLY PLANE, NOW FOUND IN EVERY WORKSHOP, WAS THE RESULT OF AMERICAN INVENTIVENESS DURING THE LAST CENTURY AND A HALF.

SAWS

The earliest saws cut by pulling~ an inefficient and inaccurate way to divide wood. The relatively soft blades of copper, brass and wrought iron would buckle and crack if the saw was pushed (not until the fourteenth century were steel furnaces able to provide a strong even temper). The ingenious Romans either reinforced the blade or held it taut in a framework for the preferred pushing cut. Not only that, but they avoided blade breakage by spreading alternate teeth in opposite directions. The wider cut needed no enlarging with wedges as in earlier days.

The teeth of the saw defined its use. Crosscut blades held a row of small triangular knives for cutting across the wood grain. Ripsaw teeth were sharpened into tiny chisels to shove out a cut with the grain. Small and large unframed saws were either crosscut or rip. Framed saws limited the scope of the cut. The Romans used the bowsaw and the bucksaw for crosscutting. But there were later small framed saws such as the turning saw and then the coping saw that had rip teeth. Large framed saws, hindered by the frame, could only rip down the grain of the timber.

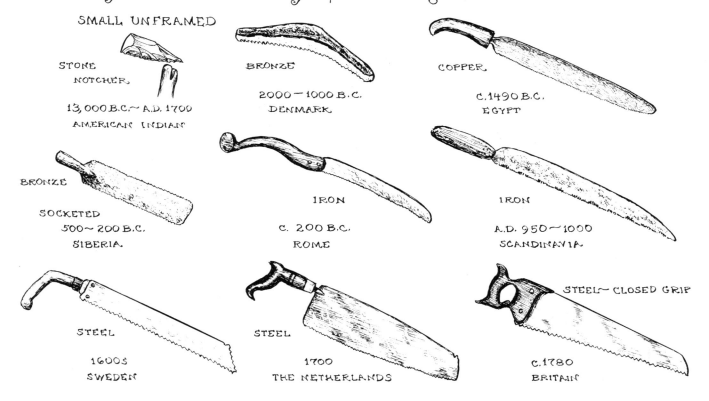

SMALL UNFRAMED

STONE NOTCHER
13,000 B.C.~ A.D. 1700
AMERICAN INDIAN

BRONZE
2000~1000 B.C.
DENMARK

COPPER
C.1490 B.C.
EGYPT

BRONZE
SOCKETED
500~200 B.C.
SIBERIA

IRON
C. 200 B.C.
ROME

IRON
A.D. 950~1000
SCANDINAVIA

STEEL
1600s
SWEDEN

STEEL
1700
THE NETHERLANDS

STEEL~ CLOSED GRIP
C.1780
BRITAIN

112

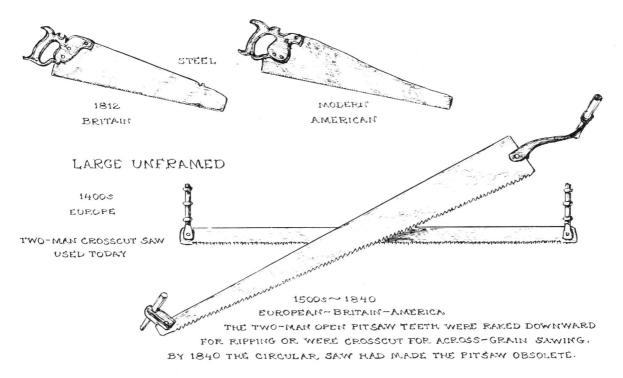

STEEL

1812
BRITAIN

MODERN
AMERICAN

LARGE UNFRAMED

1400s
EUROPE

TWO-MAN CROSSCUT SAW
USED TODAY

1500s ~ 1840
EUROPEAN ~ BRITAIN ~ AMERICA
THE TWO-MAN OPEN PITSAW TEETH WERE RAKED DOWNWARD
FOR RIPPING OR WERE CROSSCUT FOR ACROSS-GRAIN SAWING.
BY 1840 THE CIRCULAR SAW HAD MADE THE PITSAW OBSOLETE.

SMALL FRAMED

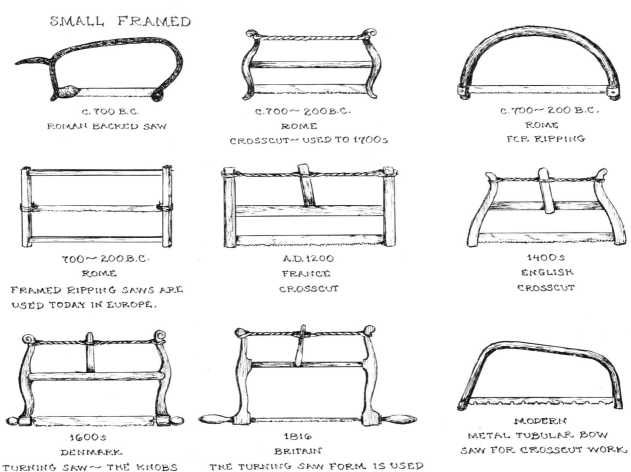

C. 700 B.C.
ROMAN BACKED SAW

C. 700 ~ 200 B.C.
ROME
CROSSCUT ~ USED TO 1700s

C. 700 ~ 200 B.C.
ROME
FOR RIPPING

700 ~ 200 B.C.
ROME
FRAMED RIPPING SAWS ARE
USED TODAY IN EUROPE.

A.D. 1200
FRANCE
CROSSCUT

1400s
ENGLISH
CROSSCUT

1600s
DENMARK
TURNING SAW ~ THE KNOBS
TURNED THE RIPPING BLADE.

1816
BRITAIN
THE TURNING SAW FORM IS USED
TODAY IN NORTHERN EUROPE.

MODERN
METAL TUBULAR BOW
SAW FOR CROSSCUT WORK

LARGE FRAMED

WEDGED BLADE IN IRON SLINGS

ANOTHER WAY TO
WEDGE THE BLADE

PITMAN'S
HANDLE

SAWYER'S
HANDLE

1600s
EUROPE AND THE AMERICAN COLONIES

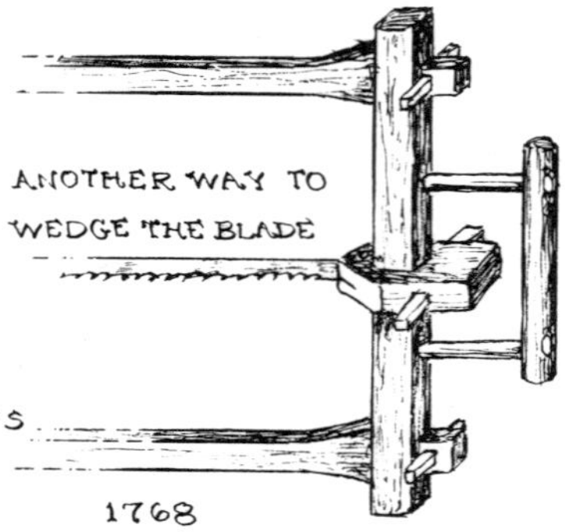

1768
FRANCE

THE TWO-MAN FRAMED PITSAW, LIKE SO MANY OTHER WOODWORKING TOOLS, ORIGINATED WITH
THE ROMANS. OVER THE CENTURIES, ITS RIPSAW BLADE TURNED OUT COUNTLESS MILES OF BOARDING.
THE LABOR-INTENSIVE FRAMED PITSAW WAS REPLACED BY THE WATER-POWERED SAWMILL, THEN THE
UNFRAMED (OPEN) PITSAW, AND FINALLY THE CIRCULAR SAW.

Bibliography

Bailey, Kenneth Holmes. *Masonry*. The Home Mechanic's Library. New York: D. Van Nostrand Company, 1945.

Barlow, Ronda S. *The Antique Tool Collector's Guide to Value*. El Cajon, Calif.: Windmill Publishing Company, 1989.

Bealer, Alex W. *Old Ways of Working Wood*. Rev. ed. Barre, Mass.: Barre Publishing Co., 1980.

———. *The Art of Blacksmithing*. 3rd ed. Revised and updated by Charles McRaven. New York: Harper & Row, 1984.

Benson, Tedd, with James Gruber. *Building the Timber Frame House: The Revival of a Forgotten Craft*. New York: Scribner, 1980.

Blackburn, Graham. *Illustrated Housebuilding*. Woodstock, N.Y.: The Overlook Press, 1974.

Blandford, Percy W. *Country Craft Tools*. New York: Funk & Wagnalls, 1976.

Cummings, Abbott Lowell. *Architecture in Early New England*. Old Sturbridge Village Booklet Series. Old Sturbridge, Inc., 1984.

Diderot, Denis. *L'Encyclopédie ou Dictionnaire Raisonné des Arts et des Métiers*. Paris,1751–1765.

Eldin, H. L. *Woodland Crafts in Britain*. England: Newton Abbot, David & Charles, 1973.

Elliott, Stewart. *The Timber Frame Planning Book*. Chicago: Contemporary Books, 1978.

Goodman, W. L. *The History of Woodworking Tools*. London: G. Bell and Sons, 1964.

Hamilton, Edward P. *The Village Mill in Early New England*. Old Sturbridge Village Booklet Series. Old Sturbridge, Inc., 1964.

Heuvel, Johannes. *The Cabinetmaker in Eighteenth-Century Williamsburg*. Williamsburg Craft Series. Colonial Williamsburg, 1963.

Isham, Norman Morrison. *Early American Houses: The Seventeenth Century*. Classic Guide Books to the Visual Arts. Watkins Glen, N.Y.: American Life Foundation, 1968.

———. *A Glossary of Colonial Architectural Terms*. Watkins Glen, N.Y.: American Life Foundation, 1968.

Isham, Norman M., and Albert F. Brown. *Early Connecticut Houses*. New York: Dover, 1965.

Kauffman, Henry J. *American Axes*. Brattleboro, Vt.: Stephen Greene Press, 1972.

———. *Early American Ironware: Cast and Wrought*. New York: Weathervane Books, 1966.

Kebabian, Paul B., and Dudley Whitney. *American Woodworking Tools*. Boston: New York Graphic Society, 1978.

Kelly, J. Frederick. *Early Domestic Architecture of Connecticut*. New York: Dover, 1963.

Kettell, Russell Hawes, ed. *Early American Rooms*. New York: Dover, 1967.

Kimball, Fiske. *Domestic Architecture of the American Colonies and of the Early Republic*. New York: Dover, 1966.

Labine, Clem, and Carolyn Flaherty, eds. *The Old-House Journal Compendium*. Woodstock, N.Y.: The Overlook Press, 1980.

Lindsay, J. Seymour. *Iron and Brass Implements of the English and American House*. Bass River, Mass.: Carl Jacobs, 1964.

Martin, Thomas. *The Circle of the Mechanical Arts*. London, 1813.

McKee, Harley J. *Introduction to Early American Masonry*. Washington, D.C.: National Trust for Historic Preservation, 1973.

Mercer, Henry Chapman. *Ancient Carpenter's Tools*. 3rd ed. Doylestown, PA: Bucks County Historical Society, 1960.

Morrison, Hugh. *Early American Architecture*. (from the First Colonial Settlements to the National Period). New York: Oxford University Press, 1952.

Moxon, Joseph. *Mechanic Exercises*. 3rd ed. London, 1703.

Mullins, Lisa C., ed. *Colonial Architecture of the Mid-Atlantic*. Vol. IV. Architectural Treasures of Early American Series. A publication of the National Historical Society. Pittstown, N.J.: Main Street Press, 1987.

Nicholson, Peter. *The Mechanic's Companion*. Philadelphia, 1832.

Pain, William. *The Builder's Companion and Workman's General Assistant*. London: printed for the author and Robert Sayer at the Golden Buck in Fleet Street, 1762.

Peterson, Harold L. *American Indian Tomahawks*. New York: Museum of the American Indian, Hoye Foundation, 1965.

Peterson, Harold L. *American Knives*. New York: Scribner, 1958.

Pool, J. Lawrence, and Angeline J. Pool, eds. *America's Valley Forces and Valley Furnaces*. Dalton, Mass.: 1982.

Poor, Alfred Easton. *Colonial Architecture of Cape Cod*. New York: Dover, 1970.

Salaman, R. A. *Dictionary of Woodworking Tools c. 1700–1970 and Tools of Allied Trades*. Rev. ed. Newtown, Conn.: Taunton Press, 1990.

Sayward, Elliot M., ed. *The Chronicle*. Early American Industries Association, 1933.

Sloane, Eric. *A Museum of Early American Tools*. New York, W. Funck, 1964.

———. *A. Reverence for Wood*. New York: W. Funck, 1965.

Smith, Elmer L. *Early Tools and Equipment*. Lebanon, Pa.: Applied Art Publishers, 1974.

Sobon, Jack, and Roger Schroeder. *Timber Frame Construction: All about Post-and-Beam Building*. A Garden Way Publishing Book. Pownal, Vt.: Storey Communications, 1984.

Tumis, Edwin. *Colonial Craftsmen and the Beginnings of American Industry*. Cleveland: World Publishing Company, 1965.

Underhill, Roy. *The Woodwright's Companion*. Chapel Hill, N.C.: University of North Carolina Press, 1983.

———. *The Woodwright's Shop*. Chapel Hill, N.C.: University of North Carolina Press, 1981.

Welsh, Peter C. *Woodworking Tools 1600–1900*. Contributions from the Museum of History and Technology: Paper 51 (178–228). Washington, D.C.: Smithsonian Institution, 1966.

Weygers, Alexander G. *The Making of Tools*. New York: Van Nostrand Reinhold Company, 1973.

Wigginton, Eliot. *The Foxfire Book*. Garden City, N.Y.: Anchor Books, Doubleday, 1972.

Wildung, Frank H. *Woodworking Tools at Shelburne Museum*. Museum Pamphlet Series, Number 3. Shelburne, Vt.: Shelburne Museum, 1957.

Williams, Henry Lionel, and Ottalie K. Williams *Old American Houses 1700–1850*. New York: Bonanza Books, 1967.

Wyatt, Edwin M. *Common Woodworking Tools: Their History*. Milwaukee: Bruce Publishing Company, 1936.

Index

About the Author

A retired medical doctor, C. Keith Wilbur has written seven titles in the *Illustrated Living History Series*, including *New England Indians*, *Revolutionary Medicine*, and *Indian Handcrafts* (all Globe Pequot). He and his wife, Ruth, a retired museum director, live in Northampton, Massachusetts.